A DOUGHBOY'S NARRATIVE

COM-SE   COM-SAE

BY
A DOUGHBOY
SAMUEL DAVID SPIVEY

D1275076

A DOUGHBOY'S NARRATIVE

DEDICATION

To my wife Euvida, who has always gone the extra mile to do for me and give me her support. To my children, James, Cathy, Debbie, and my Grandchildren, Andrew, Ben (Benjamin), Meredith, and Erin. They make life worth living for us. And my family who give me their love, their support, so that we may feel and express our mutual devotion. To my Doughboy Comrades of Company "E" 26 Infantry Regiment. Most of all the four thousand three hundred twenty five men of THE BIG RED ONE that gave it all.

ACKNOWLEDGEMENTS

A special thanks to Rose Mary and Tom Spivey for their successful typing of the long hand scribbles that made the Narrative readable.

Several people made significant contributions to this Narrative. I thank them wholeheartedly.

Rodney and Shirley L'Amoureux, for their expertise in editing portions of the Narrative. A hearty "WELL DONE" to Rod for his comments that are included in the Narrative.

Mike Spiegel for the appropriately designed and wonderfully pleasing cover.

Hilda Brodrick and Lydia Rensch for typing and transcribing portions of the Narrative.

Bobby Moye for his encouragement and much advice on various topics.

To the contributors of stories in the Appendix; 1, Colonel Belisle, Appendix 2, CWO4 Manning, and Appendix 3, S/Sgt. DeWitte. What a wonderful feeling it is to know that you cared. I THANK YOU very, very, much.

A special "Thanks" to all my Reunion buddies of Company "E", just for what you are, heros and comrades. You have helped me tremendously in remembering joyful events, and the hellish horrors of the life of a Doughboy in combat. There is no way that I can completely explain many of these events. These Friends are instrumental in arousing my interest and made "A Doughboy's Narrative" a reality.

ABOUT THE AUTHOR

Samuel David Spivey was born six September nineteen twenty-four in Canoe, Alabama. Orphaned was when he was eight and lived with share-cropper relatives until February nineteen forty. Sam enlisted in the United States Army at the young age of fifteen, at Mobile, Alabama. He was sent to Fort Benning, Georgia, and was assigned to the First Infantry Division that was at Fort Benning temporarily on maneuvers. He was trained for the Infantry, as a rifleman, later specializing in mortars and light machine guns. Sam served in Africa and Europe in World War II in the First Infantry Division, and in the Third Infantry Division in the Korean War. He retired from the Army in June nineteen of sixty-five as a Command Sergeant Major. Since retiring from the Army he has made his home in Atlanta, Albany, Marietta, and back to Albany, Georgia.

(Cathy Spivey Barrett) I remember when I first asked my dad to write down his impressions of WWII and the events which were memorable to him. I never thought that it would develop into a book. I am so happy and proud to have the opportunity to express to others how much my father, has affected my life. Dad made me what I am. As far back as I remember my dad was a devoted, loving, and generous father. Not only was he a positive role model to me, Dad took the time to enjoy his children and be a part of their lives. My Dad took the time to go camping and travel to many places of interest to us. He helped us with our homework, (as much as he could), attended piano concerts and special church events.

He was present when my two children, Ben and Meredith were born. Now that I am a parent, I can appreciate the devotion Dad consistently expressed to us. These qualities my father exemplifies have contributed to what I want to instill in my own children. To live each day to it's fullest, taking time to enjoy what you have, cherish those you love, and not to have any regrets. Forever I will be grateful for being blessed with such a wonderful father who has made such an important impact on me. This book is invaluable to me because through this book my children and grandchildren will know him and see the patriotic American and Christian that he is. For this I feel so proud of him.

(James David Spivey, Master Sergeant United States Army Retired) When my father asked me to write something maybe to use in the introduction in his narrative, my first reaction was, "Why, would someone want their son to write an introduction?" In the days following my father's request an incident was on **Cable News Network** that enforced his request. **CNN** had reported a child abuse case and the divorce of the parents; the child abuse, molestation was instrumental in this tragic breakup of a family. This made me think of how much I appreciate and love my parents. I know that I have much to be thankful for. Such as, loving parents. I regret that in my earlier years, especially teenage and twenties, that I was not a better son. Seeing kids grow up today, I see allot of me in them and it saddens me to see that young people do not have more love and respect for their parents.

Like my father I to undertook a career in the U. S. Army. His influence over me has been a credit to my success in the United States Army Special Operations community. Not only do I owe my father a lot for this, but so does the country.

How grateful I am that he survived the rigors of World War II, for if he had not, I would not be here. Nor would I ever have the thought of having different parents, for because of their love and guidance, I have been able to be a successful adult. It is a credit to my parents that they have three children that have not been a lifetime burden. I am truly grateful.

(Debbie Spivey Lunsford) When my father comes to mind, it is a feeling I get about myself when I am with him or think of him. As opposed to words or phrases that describe him. His personality and beliefs have enabled me to become the person I am. He has enabled me to develop confidence in my abilities to be liked, capable, and worthy. He has ingrained a strong sense of morality, integrity, and responsibility. My father has given me fond memories of a loving family, pride in my accomplishments and self, a sense of caring for others, and a respect for truth. I guess the beliefs with which he has gifted me, he contains and abides by in his own life. Thanks Dad. Congratulations on fulfilling your dream in the writing of this book. I love you.

(Reverend Bobby Moye) Sam is fiercely dedicated to his Comrades, and has spent much time seeking to memorialize the marvelous feats and accomplishments of the First Infantry Division and those who served during World War II. Sam is a committed Military Man who has not and cannot forget the supreme price and ultimate sacrifice by this Country's finest young Soldiers who gave all, that we might have all.

God give us more men who are patriotic and love their Country like Sam. He is strong on Spiritual values which make America what it ought to be. Sam Spivey and his wife, Euvida have two lovely daughters and one fine son and, are also blessed with four grandchildren.

One and all will find inspiration and motivation, and blessings to carry on great Military tradition in this, A DOUGHBOY'S NARRATIVE

FORWARD

As I have tried to write something that might be of interest to various people it has not been an easy task. In some ways, it has been fun, exhilarating, and a challenge. If only I had known earlier in life the value of a journal, diary, letters or anything besides just shooting off from the top of my head, it might have been much easier. Many years ago I was told that I did not have to worry about having a heart attack, for I did not have a heart nor emotion. Things have changed, as I was trying to remember various happenings, particularly the exploits of my buddies and friends, I became very emotional. It just plain hurts. Especially the personal part of reminiscing about these buddies and friends, who were very much a part of my life; and yes, I am very emotional.

Looking back over my life I have had many abrupt changes. A mixture of some very pleasant and beneficial, and some of a horrible, and regrettable nature. I do not care to elaborate on the unpleasant exploits. I feel that it would not serve any purpose in enhancing this story. Nor will I write much about some of the gut wrenching incidents that I have tried to forget. They still are so sad and emotional that I do not care to dwell on them. I am very grateful for the many good things that made my life worth living, especially for the love of a wonderful family, and the good life, past and present. My greatest regret is that at times I was not able to provide my loving wife and children things that they deserved and needed, and to some extent, what they wanted.

I have tried very hard to keep events in order as much as possible. It is not my wish to make my role or the role of others look larger than it was; Nor to make me or others look better than we were. What I have written is real, first hand as I remember and some of the incidents are even toned down a bit. It is impossible for me to put into words many of the unbelievable actions of the Doughboys; such as their daring, their exploits that seem to come natural, and the impossible tasks performed by units of the RED ONE. Another impossible task, is to tell in a convincing way the misery a Doughboy faces daily. I agree with whoever said, if one is a hero you don't have to tell anyone; or if one is good, people will know it.

I have not been too kind in my opinions of some Officers and Noncommissioned Officers who I knew. Neither will I apologize for criticizing. The greatest of joy is I have served with some of the best ever. To the many good soldiers (enlisted men) who did what they were asked, and did it well; and, to the many good soldiers who kept me on track with their understanding and guidance, which made me look better than I was. THANKS.

Most of my family that I know or knew, were Christians. During the war I was not religious, I had no feelings for religion and was indifferent, God was not a part of my life. Though I was indifferent to God, still due to my heritage and traditions taught to me by my family, I know now, that God was with me. In the turmoil of a fight, I would shout at the men, "move, do this or that, we're not going to die, because, we are too mean to die. God don't want us, and the devil wouldn't have us." I never attended church services, nor prayed, or asked God to watch over me. All during the campaigns, I depended on Sam, my team mates, and buddies. But oh, how things change. Now He is in every part of my life. I see the miracles past and present. There is just no way that I could have survived without God's interventions. I was bitter about the loss of my father and mother (at age five and eight). If God loved me, He would not have taken them. How could I be so wrong? All these many years of my young life, I was seeking, but not finding fulfillment in life. God, Jesus, one and the same, gives me the abundant joy of living. For many years I didn't drop the misfortunes of my early life. And now I turn everything over to God that I can't handle, try not to worry about the things that I cannot change, and have hope for the best.

I would have liked to have been able to give the much deserved credits to my buddies, my friends and others. I am unable to properly identify many of them, nor can I remember all of the details of their exploits. To all a heartfelt THANKS, given with the love that only Comrades know.

I know that some who read this narrative will wonder why I waited fifty years to write about these events. Shortly after leaving the combat area, a questionnaire was sent to me that asked "What was my opinion about the war, and what were my thoughts about returning to civilian life." My answer was very short, "I just wanted to be left alone and live my life, and to forget all about it, (the war)." That feeling stayed with me for some forty years, and I did not talk much about the war and tried to forget. I still have a choke factor about incidents of combat even to this day. As time passed, I became aware of how little people knew about World War II. The Department of Defense has a program to inform the American People of the events and people of World War II. I became interested in the program and started an informant program at my church, Sunnyside Baptist. As a result, I started writing about what I remembered about life of years gone by. I had been thinking about writing something. I made a start some years ago at the request of family members and others, and particular by my daughter, Cathy. So "A Doughboy's Narrative" became a reality for my family and Comrades of Company "E" 26th Infantry and, "The Big Red One." The Narrative is a mixture, a little of this, a little of that, neither good, neither bad, in other words, I believe the French saying is, "COM-SE, COM-SAE." My hope is that it will be of interest.

I think mentioning a little about the First Infantry Division and laying a little groundwork is in order. In a very convincing way, I would like to tell some of what we learned, what we believed, what we did, and how we felt. The name, "THE BIG RED ONE," "THE FIGHTING FIRST," the history, the tradition, the pride, is second to none. I am going to mention actions of the men and the Division's achievements in World War II. We must understand and believe that traditions are the guts of morale. We have to believe that we are the best damned Squad, Platoon, Company, Battalion, Regiment, and Division in the whole damned army. As history speaks to us now, we know we were. We were no different than any American, yet we had to believe we were the best. This belief and training, is what makes the First Division what it was, and is, second to none. The First Division has streamers, awards, historical achievements, first in just about everything. Exploits of the Big Red One are axioms. We also have a comradeship that is impossible to explain or define. Feelings of "One for All," and "All for One" is all inclusive. The First Division's mottos are, "No Mission Too Difficult, No Sacrifice Too Great, Duty First." And after losing thousands in a battle in WW1 this phrase was repeated, "It's not for me to ask why, but to do or die," that's what we lived or died by. Also the Division was blessed to have had great leaders who pushed us to understand the meaning of the traditions, and togetherness, and they understood the logic of the doughboy.

Let's take a stroll through The Hall of Fame of the First Division, not forgetting the long days and nights of hard strenuous, tiring, over and over training that never ended. We have a mixture of sometimes confused, and bewildered soldiers; a bit unprepared, who made the successful invasion of North Africa that started the Division's exploits in WWII. Then on to Tunisia, the piecemeal commitment into combat of the units, tactical mistakes, and just plain stupidity at times. We were fortunate, most of us survived. Beginning at El Guetter, was the first time the Division had assembled and fought in WWII as a division. By the end of the brutally hard Tunisian campaign The First Division had reached the status of an elite fighting unit. Sicily, a grueling, and one of the bloodiest of fights, is where the tradition of always taking the objective, and holding it was upheld. At Troino, "E" Company was counterattacked thirteen times, yet they still held the position with only a few remaining fighters.

More training, then Normandy, the world renowned accomplishments at Omaha, Collerville, Balleroy, and Caumont, the deepest penetration of the entire beachhead. The breakthrough near St. Lo, and the mad rush through France with deadly clashes that destroyed or cut to pieces several German Divisions in Northern France and at Moms. First into Germany, first through the fortifications (Siegfried Line) of Germany, first to take a German city, on and on. The bloody fight and horrifying losses in the Hurtgen Forest. The steadfast stance of, I won't be moved, in the Battle of The Bulge; during the German breakthrough this stance prevented the Germans from turning the U. S. Army's northern shoulder and capturing the supply depots at Liege and Verviers.

Lets not forget the taking back of ground lost during the Battle of The Bulge and then on to the Roer River. The clashes through the Roer and Rhine Valleys to the Rhine River, and The Red One crossed the Rhine 16 March 1945. The bitter clashes to enlarge the Remagen bridgehead, and the closing of the Harmon Pocket. In two months Company "E" 26th Infantry averaged losing more than five men daily. Finally to the Hartz Mountains and entry into Czechoslovakia, the end of WWII for the "RED ONE." There is no satisfactory way to end the telling of the exploits of the First Division. The costs were great, in four hundred forty three days of combat, over five thousand killed and missing, over fifteen thousand wounded in action.

The German losses were tremendous, untold tens of thousands missing and killed in action at the hands of The First Division and over one hundred thousand prisoners taken (historical fact) by The BIG RED ONE.

The magic of it's name, "The Fighting First" never retreats, always takes its objective, always moves forward, "The Big Red One" is invincible!

CHAPTER ONE
Early Years and The Fall

I have been told that the start is the most difficult in many things, I am a believer. I find that this business of writing is all very difficult. As a simple farm boy from South Alabama with a limited formal education makes writing very hard; getting my thoughts together and in order as happened and into the written form is an enormous task for me. Even after many rewrites, I find events out of order and not written with clarity. I have thought of the "early years," trying to get my thoughts of days gone by long ago. I have promised myself that I would write about what I remember and not for the way I would have liked for things to have been. Also the unpleasant and hellish happenings I will not write much about.

Tom E. Spivey 1895-1929 and Mamie B. Jernigan Spivey 1898-1933, they were parents of four boys and one girl. And in order of birth they are; Roy 8 September 1917, James 18 February 1919, Ray 15 November 1921, Margie 3 September 1922, Samuel (me) 6 September 24. Frances

8 April 1932, my half sister, was fathered by Mama's second husband, Zeb Nichols. The five Spiveys were born on a farm about a mile from Canoe, Alabama. Our home was a large "L" shaped house, about three feet off the ground with three bedrooms, large sitting and bedroom combination with fireplace, kitchen and dining room. A front porch, a rear porch between the house and dining room, and a porch the length of the kitchen and dining room connecting to the rear porch of the house. The house rear porch, the kitchen and dining room porch was "T" shaped and were where most of the activity was during nice weather. There was no such thing as an inside bathroom to us country folk in the 20s and 30s. Baths and particularly washing of the feet was done on the porch and as my brothers would finish washing at night they would race down the porch diving through the door onto their bed. The reason for mentioning this is that Mamma had relocated the bed with the foot facing the door. This bed was an iron frame bed with a high head frame and foot frame being above the mattress. Ray was in front of the pack this particular night, made his leap, diving toward what he thought was to land on the mattress. Instead he hit the iron tube running across the foot resulting in the loosening of teeth, blood, and much hollering. Needless to say, it was a hectic time as the extent of damage was examined and tended to, nothing really serious. With five active children around there seemed to be some sort of calamity all the time. Once we were rushing to breakfast and Ray was chasing me. As we ran into the kitchen I spun around Mamma and hit the open stove door cutting a gash on my face. There was a lot of blood, and I was hollering. Jim fainted, and most always when Jim saw blood he fainted. It took a while before things returned to normal. I still have the scar. Afternoons I would be outside waiting for my brothers and sister to come from school. School children passing by our house would want to look in my

mouth to see if the cut was all the way through, I thought I was sorta a celebrity.

I would like to say a little about family. I will try to give a brief description of the SPIVEYS and the JERNIGANS, my Mamma's maiden name. Now a little about my immediate family. I am not trying to build myself up nor anyone. In fact, self praise is sorta embarrassing. My wish is to describe my family as I know then, knowing that it is very difficult, and somewhat dangerous. I try very hard to see good in most everyone and not dwell on the unfavorable. My dad was a roughed individual and a family man. According to pictures he was a handsome fellow. He was congenial, well liked, and respected. My memory of my dad is that he was a caring man, concerned, and showed love to his family. My mom was quiet, reserved, and showed much love to family, and was attractive and likable. Sorta meek, but deliberate. My feeling today is that mom was not as firm with her children as most people were back then. As I was growing up, we talked about the past often. My brothers and sister Margie have some traits common to loners. They are not the outward, vocal, opinionated type individuals. Friendly, but not pushy, being a bit reserved. Easy to get along with, or congenial, not a rock the boat type, but certainly not an automatic follower. With an exception, very aware of family and attentive to them; maybe with only minor exception the love of God, family, and country is recognizable. Contrary to some of these descriptions above, Frances is an active, outward person with a desire to communicate. And me, just an opinionated, loud mouth, know it all. All, have much love for family and life centers around the family. I am not an expert in describing people, but I do know that a person is a mixture of traits, heritage, traditions, and we Spiveys are proud of most of ours, some might be considered odd or even curious. The Spiveys and Jernigans character are and were ordinary, I think maybe a little above.

Also, ordinary, is what we in the South know the word means, not the politically correct meaning. Most all are Christians, good citizens, recognize, respect and know heritage and tradition. All that I know of, when called to serve their country, served or volunteered and served with distinction and honor. As I think of these two families as caring devoted citizens, Christians, about average or above, and once again what we Southerners consider good, honest, proud Americans. No Audry Murphys, no Einsteins, just wholesome people. On the other side, in our family I don't know of any Jane Fondas, Ramsey Clarks, lying draft dodging Bill Clintons, nor any traitors of any sort. This is my meddling portion for today.

Being the youngest I was on the bottom of the pecking order, catching it from every one, deserving it at times I suppose. Being the youngest also had advantages for at times I got a lot of attention and of course I was teased a bit. It was a common practice back then to give young fellows (young girls too) money for their sweet tooth. I remember getting fifty cents once from a member of our church (Primitive Baptist), and a friend of the family. Mostly it was pennies or nickels, and, fifty cents was a heckava of a lot of money; it would buy a big sack of candy, chocolate kisses were five or six for one cent. This fellow church member worked for the Alga Lumber Company and according to most farmers, anyone that had a steady paycheck was rich and always had money. Farmers were lucky or very good farmers if they had any money except at harvest time. My Daddy was a moderately successful farmer, for we had some of the good life with a few luxuries.

Daddy worked very hard and that meant that the rest of the family also worked hard, long days. Margie and I were too young to contribute and probably were a hindrance to the others. An indication of hindrance is one day Margie and I tipped over the safe (cupboard) that we used to store milk, bread, cakes, and cookies. The goodies that we wanted were on the top shelf. We pushed a chair against the safe and started climbing. Of course it became top heavy, tipped over, spilling milk and everything else. Mamma heard the crash, came to see what was happening, caught Margie, and she got paddled, and like a smart aleck, I ran and got under the house. It would have been better if Mama had caught me, for when Daddy got home he gave me a razor strap whipping. If one ever got a razor strap whipping, it will always be remembered. I don't remember Daddy ever whipping me hard, but it was scary.

Daddy's cash crop items were cotton, strawberries, peas, potatoes, and vegetables for the family and feed for the livestock. We hear now that these were "the good old days" and they were. Life to us as a family was very good compared to later years, it indeed was, "the good old days." All the credit must go to my dad, mom and brothers to make it such a wonderful period for they worked very hard and by no means was it an easy life. To show just how hard people worked on the farm, as an example; in addition to taking care of the family and the house, Mamma did the milking, fed the chickens and most of the livestock, took care of the garden and flowers; she also worked in the fields. There never seem to be sufficient hands to do all that had to be done. The strawberry crop of 1929 was very large and Mamma helped pick them for the market. Mamma took me to the field with her, and after a short time I had a belly full of eating and picking. Mamma picked the large select strawberries that would be placed on top of the containers for looks, this made them very inviting to the buyers. I suppose that is how and why the saying of, don't purchase a pig in a poke (sack), got started from such practices. With plenty of just good old country eating, farm life was great, I think I would still love it, I try to remember the good days of back then and try to forget the bad ones. My Daddy was what you would call a go-getter. We were very fortunate to have someone to provide for us so well. We have a heck-ava lot more comforts and luxury now and also more things to aggravate and worry about, I guess.

Very few farmers had an automobile in the twenties. We were the proud owners of a Model T Ford, purchased on credit. This credit purchase proved to be a tragic mistake. Shortly after getting the car Mamma was learning to drive and she hit a telephone pole on one of her practice lessons. There was extensive damage to the car, but thankfully we received only a few bumps and scratches. The car had a gadget called a "cutout" and I appointed myself the operator of this gadget because I sat in the front seat with mom and dad. I played it up big, opening and closing the valve as directed and at times at my pleasure. With the cut-out open the car was noisy and it suited us young ones just fine. When my sister and brothers were in school it was lonesome for me, and I would beg to go with them. Preschoolers were welcome to attend school occasionally with sisters or brothers, as there was no pre-school nor kindergarten. I went with them on a very cold morning and there were mud holes and ruts filled with water that was frozen. On our way to school there was many ruts suitable for skating/sliding and of course we took every opportunity we had to have fun. It also seemed that all fun has a cost; the ice broke; Margie and I got wet and very muddy. Half frozen we had to return to the house, no school that day, plus we got paddled.

Near our house was a large pond that overflowed because of much rain in South Alabama; water was just everywhere. Our barn was flooded and water was under the house. To me it looked as if the whole world was covered with water, it reminded me of the Bible story of Noah's Ark. Much later, probably early summer, Roy, Jim, and Ray went into the pond muddying it, making the fish come to the top. As the fish came up they would catch them with their hands, and throw them on the bank. It was my job to put the fish in the tub. There were also a few snakes in the muddy water. The snakes didn't seem to bother my brothers, the guardian angels were watching over them that day for sure. According to stories about Roy, Jim and Ray, I suppose they were considered very active boys. It seems that they stayed in trouble most of the time.

Daddy, Mamma, Margie and I were attending church one Saturday, (our Church services were held once a month on Saturday and Sunday). Roy, Jim, and Ray, were to take care of things while we were gone. Well, they got to arguing about which mule could pull the most. They got Daddy's new plow lines and hitched the mules together. Of course the plow lines broke, and another big, big, razor strap whipping for them. As senior adults they remember the razor strap whipping. We always had a great time at the old swimming hole, except when one day Roy, Jim, and Ray decided that it was time for me to learn to swim, (I was almost five). They threw me in deep water and I almost drowned before they got me out. To this day I am skittish of water. And another big RS whipping for the big boys. My Uncle told me that one day Daddy gave Roy, Jim, and Ray a job to shuck corn, instead they started horsing around and fighting, of course another RS whipping. So it seems that there were very active times around the Spivey's most of the time.

I must mention a few things relating to our Church. Most of the Spiveys and Jernigans were Primitive Baptist, (only adults were members), also known as Hardshell Baptist. They did not have programs for the young people, we had to sit through all these long, long sermons. The longer we sat, the hotter and bored we became. At church it was all right to be seen but not heard, and our presence was barely tolerated. Bored as we were by the long services there were many things we would rather be doing. On this particular Sunday the big boys thought about swimming. Near the Church down the hill was a large spring and the church baptistery. The big boys slipped out of the church, by crawling out the rear door. They went swimming in the church baptistery; another RS whipping. For a long time the big fellows were sorta skittish of water. Though most of the Church members were very good people, faithful and dedicated, and took very good care of their families. It's a fact, hardly ever did one hear bad things about a Hardshell Baptist. Still, the Church name, the facilities, and programs for young people, sorta matched, primitive.

One of the functions that was a big, big hit was dinner on the ground. I really believe everyone looked forward to these well attended services with dinner on the ground; they lasted about all day. The menu was not much different from what is served today. Such as, fried chicken, chicken and dumplings, and dressing, all sorts of vegetables, various kinds of homemade cakes and pies. Last, but one of the most favorite was beef hash (some called it stew beef). It was beef chopped into small bits, cooked (fried) with a dab of onions and lots of black pepper. I liked it, and it was years later before I noticed that the black specks wasn't all black pepper. In the deep south during the summer we have lots and lots of gnats. Gnats love beef, need I say more. You must remember this tidbit when you read the story about the wine and cheese in chapters five and six.

Daddy, as I have said, was a good farmer and manager, or at least I thought so. He bought the model T Ford on credit from his half brother who was a car salesman; paying so much down and the rest due fall of 1929. We had a sudden turn to bad times when the stock market collapsed and the bottom fell out of the farm market that fall. No money, unable to sell our farm products, no jobs, we and most every one around went into hard times. This was the beginning of the depression for us, and things were to get much worse. When it came time for the car payment, Daddy didn't have it. Homer, Daddy's half-brother was desperate for the money owed on the car. He came to get one or the other but Daddy was not home. Homer went out to the car shed, started the car and as he was driving out the gate Mamma was trying to close it. Homer hit the gate, the gate hit Mamma causing severe bruises and scratches. Daddy was very upset that evening. That night Daddy took his shotgun and went out onto the back porch, then into the yard. I remember that I was clinging to Mamma as she pleaded to Daddy, not to shoot himself. Mama's pleading was to no avail, Daddy shot himself and was critically wounded. He was still able to leave the yard and go up the fence line about a hundred yards or so. Mamma, with the help of Roy and Jim were able to get Daddy back to the house. The doctor came, but was not able to do much for him. My Daddy died a day or so later with pneumonia and the gunshot wound killing him. (One of Daddy's brothers killed himself and another attempted to shoot themselves, sometimes I felt that I did not have much to look forward to). After that we entered another world, a world of uncertainty, not knowing where we were to live, never enough of the essentials.

We moved off the farm to Canoe, Alabama, into a large house with a hall down the center. A short time after we moved there I had a nightmare; I met Daddy in the hall and talked to him, it was very real to me. I thought that my Daddy was back with us, it seemed real that I was full of happiness, joy, and excitement. I soon began to realize that Daddy was not back with us and would not be back. The bitter disappointment, sadness, and the anger in my heart lingered. It took many years before I accepted the fact that God is a loving God. Back then my reasoning was that if God loved me He would not have taken my mom and dad. It was hell living my life with this bitterness, without the Church and without God, depending only on Sam. I desperately missed the presence of mom and dad, and not knowing it then, but God also.

During this time the hard, hard life began for us Spiveys that seemed to last forever. A life of just existing, never enough food, clothing, a place live, no school supplies. You name it, we didn't have it. I know that we suffered for the essentials. I knew, and know now that we were the have-nots of these times. Poor without much of a future, or so we thought. Other people were having a hard time also, the depression touched just about everyone, and our family and neighbors were not able to help. It seemed as if they thought it was best just to overlook things that they were not able to do anything about.

My Mama got a job at a cafe and boarding house at Flomaton, Alabama, about ten miles from Canoe, Alabama. She worked long hours and at night. I hardly ever remember her being at home, (she slept in the daytime), nor do I remember much about Roy, Jim, Ray, and Margie. They were in school and Roy and Jim worked at a bowling alley evenings and nights. We lived next to the railroad switch yards, so I watched trains. Flomaton was a fuel, water, and crew change stop, and there was always enough to keep my interest. I also went to school with my brothers and sister occasionally. I was old enough to attend school but I don't know why I wasn't enrolled. I got a late start and I don't think that I ever caught up.

Jim or Ray got into a fight because some boys were making fun of us for the way we looked, ragged, no shoes, our have-not status showed and we were ridiculed. It wasn't long before all of us were fighting. I'm telling this just as an indication of how we stuck together and we are still a very close family. Mamma got a better job as a cook for the railroad track repair crew, and she was gone about all the time then. The crew moved around a lot and they lived in converted box cars and children were not allowed to dwell on the work train. It is a mystery to me as to what we did when Mamma was gone on the work train. I suppose that the older boys watched after us.

Sometime in 1931 we moved to Atmore, Alabama where Mamma worked for a family as a cook and housekeeper. We lived in a small tenant house close to the main house, and we liked living there. Mamma cooked for them and they would give her things for Margie and me. Roy, Jim, and Ray lived with Mamma's parents, her brother, and her sister. Mamma started dating Zeb Nichols, a brother to Mamma's sister's husband. A few months later they got married and you would think that life would improve, but it didn't. We lived in an old rundown abandoned house way out in the woods between Wabeek and Flomaton. Roy, Jim and Ray came back to live with us, and the family was together again, which was the last time we lived in the same house together as a family. The togetherness didn't work. In many cases it seems that stepchildren cannot accept a stepparent. Roy, Jim, and Ray went back to live with Mamma's relatives. Shortly we moved again, and into an old one room schoolhouse on the main road. It was maybe about 20x28, not much room for a family of five. Here at least we had neighbors and not way out in the woods away from everyone and everything.

The school year of 1931 and 1932 was the year I started attending school, and it was only for part of the year and I did not pass. Fall of 1932 was my first full year of a sort attending school, I was eight years old. Quite a late start. My reckoning is that I started with two strikes against me; and, I never seemed to have caught up. As the hard life became worse, it was very hard to scrape up enough to eat; no new clothes and shoes nor money for books, paper, and pencils. This was the norm for us that started after Daddy died and was with us all my young life. Times were so bad that we considered ourselves lucky if we didn't go to be bed hungry, which we did quite often. Zeb, my stepdaddy, was hooked on booze and everything that he could borrow or beg was spent on booze. I do not remember him ever contributing anything for the benefit of the family. Mamma had a purebred sow left from what we had on the farm when Daddy was living. This sow got on the railroad track and was killed. The railroad paid Mamma for the sow. Zeb, by some means, got the money, went to Flamaton and did not come back until it was all spent and nothing to show for it.

The government had programs that helped some, such as it was, which was a very small amount. But mostly it was handouts and hand-me-downs. My recollection of the government welfare is slim to nil judged on what we received. Also back then people didn't expect help, and as the saying goes, root hog or die poor was their way of life. I believe that some didn't much care if things were better or not; they were confused, beaten down, and just didn't care. For the lack of a better explanation I believe that most country people around where we lived did not question much about their status in life. When they were in poverty with nothing, without sufficient food and other essentials, they just accepted it as if it was their fate. In other words most did not exert their brains to try to figure out a better way. Kinda reminds me of dumb animals, this statement is worse than cruel, I hate to say it. It was a fact, some land owners would cheat the tenant farmers, give them just enough to barely live, and always keeping them in debt. The tenant farmer would stay year after year, accepting it as a way of life, or their fate. My Uncle Bennie tried to tell Papa that he was being cheated, yet Papa stayed year after year, always in debt. Uncle Bennie gave up and moved back to Texas. Papa was an excellent farmer and would have done well if this system of over charging and keeping tenant farmers in debt could have been eliminated. This way of life also applied to Uncle Gip (Daddy's brother).

All farmers that I knew that owned their land, and those that rented or leased land outright, had a much better standard of living than a sharecropper. (Sharecropper farmers are those that farmed on halves or shares).

A Doughboys Narrative ●

CHAPTER TWO
Hard Times and The Struggle

M y sister Frances was born during the hardest of times, April nineteen thirty-two. Margie and I (age nine and seven) would babysit when Mamma was out trying to gather something to eat; getting vegetables that neighbors and friends would give her, most always she would have to get them out of our friend's garden and fields. At times I would babysit alone when Margie helped Mamma. Comparing times, (which I cannot help but to do so) we are very, very well off now. I think that maybe this little incident will give you an idea, or amuse, or make you wonder about as to what hard times were like in South Alabama in the early thirties. My Aunt was starting to cook dinner when she discovered that she did not have a match to start a fire. She sent one of the older children to a nearby country store for a penny box of matches; having no money she asked that the matches be charged. The store owner refused to sell a penny box of matches to her on credit. Before my aunt could cook dinner she had to wait for one of the hens to lay an egg to trade for a one cent box of matches. Now to me that is poor. Now the sad part is that this condition was wide spread, and yet, it seemed that we were on the bottom. As hard as times were, it got worse.

When my Mamma got sick, I did not know what the illness was, I do know that they did not take her to a doctor nor to a hospital because we did not have the money. They thought, no money, no treatment. There was probably a way to get treatment but no one knew how to make it happen. During WWII I recall a few times when men died of wounds because we were unable to get aid to them. As they died, I would think of my Mamma; for the lack of treatment she died, and it still hurts. My Mamma died 22 February 1933, two days before her 35th birthday. Another part of our world ended, with many, many uncertainties ahead of us. Margie, Frances, (ten months old) and I had to be taken care of by someone. Roy, Jim and Ray were already with relatives of Mamma's. It was decided that Zeb's sister would take Frances, all her young days she had a sad, deprived and depressed life. Margie and I would live with our grandparents the Jernigans, until someone would take us. The Jernigans who had already raised a family of four girls, three boys, and one infant child that died. It was indeed a sad day when we took my Mamma to our Church in a home made coffin on Papa's wagon. There is no way that I can describe the lonely, hopeless, empty feeling.

After the funeral, Papa and others of the family went by where we lived, (the old one-room schoolhouse) to get my Mamma's things, which were not much. They loaded the wagon and were just about ready to start toward Papa and Grandma's home at Robinsonville, Alabama; when, Zeb sent word that we were not to take my Mamma's things. He also said he was up the road at his brother's house with a shotgun to make sure that we didn't take anything. I did not then, and still don't understand

Zeb's reason for this, because he was not a violent person; He was a kind gentle man as I knew him. Having a drinking problem, and not providing for his family, I suppose, were his largest faults. In fact the whole Nichols clan was good natured and good to us. That threat with the shotgun upset us all, especially Grandma. Bennie, my Uncle, (my Mamma's brother), was the stubborn determined type and he took this threat as a challenge to him and he was determined to go up the road where Zeb was. Grandma was upset and pleaded for Bennie not to go by where Zeb was, but to go another way. Bennie insisted that he was going the way he usually went, and he did. There were some hard words, threats and ill feelings, but no one was shot.

Later, Papa wrote Uncle Gip, (Daddy's brother) that lived about six miles from Red Level, Alabama, to take Margie and me. Now the Spiveys were a rather large family; Daddy had ten brothers and two sisters. I had Uncles and Aunts to spare. Uncle Gip came in late spring 1933 for Margie and me. It was a strange, new home for us; we were ten and eight years old. Uncle Gip was a farmer, and a share-cropper, and life as far as luxury, did not improve. But having food was great, and a wonderful improvement. The farm land around Red Level where Uncle Gip farmed was sandy and clay where the topsoil had eroded away due to poor farming habits. Under these conditions it was difficult to make a living. It was a very meager life at its best. The so-called money crops were cotton, peanuts, (peanuts were replacing cotton due to the destructive cotton boll weevil), and cucumbers. Vegetables for our own use and of course feed for the farm animals. We had plenty to eat, such as it was.

Uncle Gip farmed a two-mule farm with his son Wilbur, and, also his wife helped; everyone helped with the farming. Last, but by no means the least, was Ruby, Uncle

Gip and Aunt Queenie's spiteful eighteen year old daughter. To me she was the most selfish, bossy, and demanding person around. Very unlikable, she made life miserable for Margie and me. Not having any diplomacy, she would try to make us do things for her. Margie and I having no reason to want to do things for her, we rebelled. She pushed us around quite a bit and to make matters worse we were not exactly a couple of angels. Nor were we the type to be pushed, we were defiant to some extent I am sure.

Seven people living in a three-room house were a bit crowded, there were two bedrooms; one was a combination bedroom/sitting-room with a fireplace. One narrow room along the back of the house was the kitchen and dining room. The most important thing was to manage to keep enough food. Farmers and especially sharecroppers had a problem doing this at times. We had a rather meager life, enough food such as it was; the menu was rather short. Most everything we ate came off the farm. Vegetables, dried beans and peas, sometimes milk and butter, cornbread, sweet potatoes, syrup and sometimes chicken. It was a never ending problem to get flour to make biscuits for breakfast. Biscuits were considered high on the hog living and a status symbol. We never ate beef and very little pork. It took too much of the valuable corn, (cornbread was our lifesaver), to raise beef cattle and hogs. Our share of the corn was used for cornmeal, the life saver for many people during the depression. We tried very hard to keep at least one milk cow, but that was very hard to do considering the feed that it took to keep cows. In summer our menu was vegetables and cornbread, winter leaf vegetables, sweet potatoes, dried beans and peas, some pork and of course syrup and cornbread. Many times dried lima beans, cornbread, and sugar cane syrup would be the extent of the meal. For our school lunches most of the time we had a biscuit with syrup, or maybe a sweet potato with sausage or ham-bacon. To make a syrup biscuit, one makes a hole in the biscuit and pour in a dab of syrup. We didn't want anyone to see what we were eating, so we tried to get away from the crowd. As I think back it was a meager life. At school we had very little heat. It was normal for us to put on all the clothes we had on a cold day; not knowing anything better we were more or less contented. As always we didn't have to look very far to see people that were about as bad off as we were. There were only a few worse off.

In the Fall we had a time of plenty (if crops were good and if we received a high price for our cotton and peanuts). It was a custom that the share cropper got paid in cash for his part of the cotton seed which was about four to six dollars a bale; (sometimes it was more). A two horse farm gathered about six to ten bales of cotton. To most share-croppers fifty dollars or less is about all the cash that they would see all year. Most all share croppers stayed in debt, year after year. The land owner would advance money or credit at his store for the tenant farmer to plant and harvest the crop. Everything they gathered would go to pay off the debts; mostly to the farm owner. They hardly ever had a surplus. This small amount of cash money from the cotton seed was used to purchase a few goodies, such as canned salmon, salt fish, cheese, oil sausage and a few other things that we did not normally have. This was a one time spending, and short lived. A small amount of school items were purchased which was always low on the totem pole. So you can imagine that we did enjoy the change in menu, and most anything different was a treat.

There was always a lot of work on the farm, and especially during planting and harvest time, which seemed to be from January through December. I had to stay out of school for days or a week at a time, helping in the fields, planting or harvesting. Of course, that meant that I was just about always behind the class in my studies, ending as the dummy of the class. Being behind most of the time, it's needless to say that I wasn't a consistent "A" student, which contributed to my not being eager to go school. Also, most country people, did not put much emphasis on an education. You didn't have to have much smarts to plow a jackass. At about age eight I started attending school as regularly as possible. I did enjoy studying about other people and other countries of the world, making an "A" once in awhile; and I did well in arithmetic.

Uncle Gip and Aunt Queenie were believers in keeping in touch with family, so we visited quite a bit. Most of the time we traveled by mule and wagon, leaving on Saturday and returning on Sunday. One year Uncle Gip had a very good crop, and he received good prices for cotton and peanuts, so he bought a car, a 1930 or 31 Pontiac. Looking back, I don't think that it was wise to spend what little money we had on a car. For a while we were living high on the hog though, visiting a lot when we had money to purchase gasoline. Mostly though living conditions were tight and not much different from before we got the car. Still no new clothes, shoes or school stuff, but mostly hand-me-downs. Margie and I were not used to getting much; but, worst of all was the feeling at times that we were not wanted, or a part of the family. The visiting with our kin as we did was a good diversion and helped our feelings a lot. Aunt Queenie's relatives, plus all the Spiveys, made a large group of people with many children, and when we got together we had a wonderful time. Also I had a few friends that lived within walking distance. So life was never dull for Margie and me. Grandpa Spivey was an exception, I never did get to know my Grandpa Spivey. He was the type of person that did not show any emotion, he did not show any feeling toward Margie and me. In fact, I don't remember ever having a conversation with him, even though I saw him quite often, but being sociable wasn't his strong point.

Wilbur, Uncle Gip's son moved and Roy came and stayed with us for about a year, helping with the farming. Roy left and went to Big Spring, Texas, and worked on a widow lady's farm that we had known when they lived in Canoe, Alabama. Roy worked with her until 1940 when he went into the Army. Jim came to Uncle Gip's next to help for about a year and he also went into the Army in February 1937. When Roy and Jim (James) worked with Uncle Gip, there was no money involved; just a place to stay and something to eat. Occasionally Roy and Jim would earn a small amount helping neighbors. I suppose this was one reason that the Army looked so good to us. On account of Ruby many seemed to think that living with Uncle Gip was not good for Margie and me. Ruby, was always a bossy and selfish person, or maybe mean, and made life miserable for us. So Margie left and went back to Papa and Grandma's.

About a year later someone thought it would be better if I went back to Papa's to live. Jim, Uncle Gip, and Aunt Queenie were to be gone all day visiting with friends. On this particular Sunday I begged off from going, on the premise of visiting my friends, the Joseys. Jim was the planner of my leaving Uncle Gip's, but I thought I had the roughest part which was the leaving, for a ten year old it's hard to do. In order for Jim not to have to do any explaining he left me $1.50 in a prearranged location. Enough money for the bus ticket from Andalusia to Canoe, Alabama. The fare was $1.25 and I, had twenty-five cents for something to eat, or whatever struck the fancy of a ten year old. It was a long walk; I had expected to catch a ride, but there wasn't much traffic that day, so I had to walk about ten miles. I did not make the first bus to Canoe and the next bus left Andalusia about six p.m.. It was a very long few hours waiting on the bus, expecting Uncle

Gip to come at any moment. Uncle Gip did come looking for me, but I had left about an hour earlier.

I arrived in Canoe about ten p.m. which was six miles from Papa's. I did not know anyone in Canoe to stay with or take me to Papa's. I had to walk again, alone and at night. I suppose that my ability to walk so much was one of the reasons I made an outstanding Doughboy. The infantry always walked, walked and walked. A dark night, a little cloudy, warm and with all kinds of noises, scary things, and everything imaginable lurking around. A very scary time indeed for a ten year old, and much anxiety. What a day! Scared about leaving, scared by all the imaginary, scary things, tired from walking about ten miles that morning, plus standing, and waiting a few hours. And as I have reminisced of these times I believe that it made many things easier in later years.

Papa was a share cropper also, so the money available situation did not improve, nor the amount of work. In fact Papa could think of more things to do than just about any person that I know of. The amount of acreage planted in various crops was determined by the amount of labor available to cultivate and harvest, but they always stretched it a bit. A share cropper could not afford to hire extra help. Uncle Gip and Papa cultivated about the same acreage, the crops were different. Around Atmore where Papa lived the soil was very rich and grew abundant crops. It also took more work for this type of soil. A two-mule farm has to have two grown men just to do the cultivating. So it was Uncle Bennie for one year and the next year Uncle Bud (Papa's sons) that helped. Papa and grandma were good managers at keeping plenty to eat, canned a lot of vegetables, fruits and just about always had milk and butter, and also cured pork. So it was country eating at its best at Papa's.

Most share croppers as I have said before did not have much wealth, just honesty and plenty of work is about all that they had to brag about. Clothes, shoes, and things for school were in short supply, and as a result we kinda sorta stood out like a sore thumb. Some boys and girls, particularly at school, can be and are cruel and critical. There were others that were in the "have not" and "hand-me-down" gang, and school was not very inviting to some of us. One year, I think it was 1938, we were having a Christmas play and the teacher wanted me to play one of the parts in the play. Needing fairly decent clothes and shoes, as I had neither, I did not take the part. I felt great at being chosen, but sad because I couldn't take part.

We worked hard at planting and harvesting as I have mentioned and it was necessary for me to stay out of school for days or a week at these times. I was quite large, (tall and skinny) for my age, and I was a lot of help, such as toting seed and fertilizer to the planter and distributor. I did some cultivating and was quite capable of gathering and feeding the sugar cane mill. Always it seemed that there was water to draw and wood to tote in.

For people who have never lived on a farm, I would like to give you an idea as to what a young fellow must do, starting at a young age. There is always wood to be carried in for the cooking stove, and fireplace in the winter months. A fellow eight to twelve years old has to make many trips to fill the wood box. Then water has to be drawn for cooking, washing, and livestock. At times when it was dry, we would have to water the plants that we would set out. It's unbelievable how much water it takes, especially if you have to draw it from a well a couple of gallons at a time. It was also my job to keep the smoke going for curing the meat. Plus, feed the livestock and help in milking the cows. All these chores you do before and after school. In addition, there are many seasonal chores. I guess one of the most miserable chores is milking on a cold morning before daylight. Occasionally a cow or calf would step on your foot which is quite painful; On a cold morning it is extra painful. And the only way to get them off was to knock or push them off; that is hard to do, as they are mighty unyielding. Getting up before daylight to dust potatoes while the dew is on them is another dreadful chore. Then it is a rush to try to clean up a bit and then hurry off to school.

So much for the unpleasant chores, now the good. There would be slack times, like the lull between laying by of the crops and the harvest; sometimes after it would rain, Ray and I would rush to the creek about a mile or so from the house to fish. We both enjoyed the outdoors, and did much fishing and hunting. Once, we rushed to the creek after a heavy rain to fish, and while we were fishing, our dog, that Ray and I considered part of the family was out in the woods hunting. Pup began barking and running toward us all of a sudden; we stopped to see what was happening, we saw Old Pup followed by a herd of wild hogs. We knew that we were in big trouble. Ray picked up a stick to protect us from the hogs, I wasn't that brave so, I scooted up a tree. In just a moment, Ray realized that he would be better off up in the tree also. Then Old Pup took off when we deserted him and went back home. Old Pup was our shadow and companion. It was about a half an hour before the hogs left. Even though we were wood wise, we were kinda a bit scared, wild hogs are dangerous.

Ray and I, with our cousins and friends, would stay out in the woods hunting, fishing, or whatever, when we could from Friday evening till Sunday. We always took salt, and if we killed anything, we would roast it and have a feast. In season we would boil peanuts, swipe a watermelon or sugar cane, and slip out a bit of coffee when we could. We would build a fire, make coffee, and try to act like grownups. So with hunting bee hives, hunting small game and fishing, we stayed busy and went hunting or fishing anytime we could get off. These types of outside activities were the original "roughing it." A knife, a dab of salt, probably a stick, and a syrup can were our camping equipment. You learn a lot and there is much to learn.

My first visit to a fair or circus was a disappointment. I had just enough money to see the main event, the big Three Ring Show. The fare was probably fifty or seventy-five cents. It was many years before I learned the significance of a Three-Ring Show, sometimes country boys are slow. I got confused by the yelling, "see this, see that" and went into a side show, and afterward did not have the fare to see the main event. It was many years before I finally saw a Three-Ring Show. The first was on TV, the first live performance was in the late seventies in Atlanta. We would also work when possible for neighbors to earn our own money hoping that we would be allowed to use some for our pleasure, such as the fair. Maybe we got to go to a movie, which was very, very seldom. Going to the movie was a memorable occasion and I could count the few times I saw one before I went into the Army.

I mentioned before the many things that we raised on the farm and also that late summer and fall were the desirable times. With the abundant garden and fruits it was a time of plenty. Papa made sugar cane syrup that was the best ever, and Grandma's biscuits, jams and jellies, like the syrup, were also the best ever. Papa cured as much pork as he could, or afford. You can very well imagine why we all liked this time of year the best. A few years earlier, about 1930-33 we were not sure that we would have enough, and at times we didn't. When you really know what hard times are, then you can really appreciate times of plenty. Most of the time Papa as a share cropper did not have money for tobacco, snuff, salt, pepper, sugar, coffee and other small items. Generally we traded chickens and eggs for these, so one can image that we did not eat a lot of chicken or eggs. Neither was there money for school books, shoes, clothes. (still hand-me-downs) so this was another reason for not wanting to go to school. Luxury items such as sweet smelling soap, tooth brushes and tooth paste and many other things that we take for granted now, we did not have. I was about fourteen when I got my first tooth brush, which cost ten cents. I filled out a coupon and sent it off for my first tooth paste, a free sample tube of Ipana a very small one. It was a problem to get three cents for the stamp. Baking soda and salt was the tooth "paste" we used if we had a tooth brush. This is one item I don't think we really needed, none of us had any cavities until we entered the real world of junk food.

Sometime around 1936 while living with Papa and Grandma I was sick and had a high fever at times with nightmares. Like the time I was in the hall with Daddy when I was five. For years I had nightmares just about every time I had a high fever. I got up out of bed during the night and left the house, went to the barn, crawled under the barn and out the other side. Then I walked in my sleep to a neighbor's house about a half mile away. They heard me and found me standing outside in the chimney corner crying. I had been dreaming that some-one was chasing me; I was very frightened. After that when I was sick, someone slept with me. A short time later I had a high fever and my Aunt was sleeping with me, she woke, caught me by my shirt tail as I was going out the window onto the firewood platform. She had to get help to get me inside.

Can you imagine what it is like for a young farm boy going to town just a couple times a year? You can bet that my eyes were wide open, there were hundreds of new and strange things to get my attention. A cotton gin going full speed twenty-four hours a day, sometimes it took all day to get a bale of cotton ginned. Or watching potatoes be sorted, graded, bagged, and loaded for shipment to far off places like, Chicago, Boston, or New York. Or, take a few bags of cucumbers to the pickling plant and watch the grading, sorting and dumping into the brim (salt) tanks for the curing process. Afterwards the brimmed soaked cucumbers would be shipped way off to be packed for the stores. Going into the stores there would be unidentifiable or strange things, plus the many different odors. It was impossible for a young country boy to see all these things and the strange people and sort it all out to where it made sense. These trips also meant that you might have a few goodies, or at least some sort of new or strange things for a snack lunch, or something different. I cherish these experiences, it helps me to sorta forget the bad tines, most of all appreciate the good things of later years. I try to think of the good and try not to dwell on the bad. A great experience early morning, get up say, 3-4am to load a bale cotton; the weather cool, the sky so clear that one felt as if you could reach up and touch the harvest moon. I can see and feel these experiences as I reminisce.

Lacking most of the necessities for school I did not attend school after the sixth grade. I was thirteen when I quit, almost six feet tall and about one hundred twenty-five pounds, can you imagine how I felt in a class of much smaller children eleven and twelve years' old? School to me as a youngster was a drag and I do not have very many pleasant thoughts about my school days. I never had books, clothes, shoes as most other children had. Above all, I don't recall ever getting much encouragement to attend, study or learn. We always had to walk a few miles, which was discouraging in lousy weather, so I had many excuses not to attend. I read now of how fine they say schools were back then; I can't believe or agree that schools were as good as some say; the ones that I attended weren't. There was one teacher with thirty or forty in three or more grades, in a large room, heated by one pot bellied stove and most of the time without wood or coal. As I remember it had a lot to be desired, plus the scarcity of paper, books and such. We sat together to share books, had to try to borrow books to take home to study. I was a bit self conscious of my status as a "have not" and being much larger than my classmates made me feel rather awkward.

My Uncle Tom Nichols joined the Civil Conservation Corps early spring of 1939, and had just started breaking land on his one mule farm. My Aunt, his wife had died a few years earlier leaving her oldest daughter Ruth to take care of a younger brother and four younger sisters. I was to help her finish the breaking of ground and planting. I thought that I could do it, also it was a great opportunity for me. I went into it with great expectations, but it was not long before I learned the many facts of farming. It takes a lot of work, knowledge and continuous desire. Even with some help from the neighbors I was not able to do the amount of work needed to raise a crop. It was just about a failure. But it was also quite an experience, but nothing to show for it. It did much to improve my determination for a better vocation.

While I was living at the Nichols I missed Grandma's good eating, and wanted very much at times to go back home. My cousin William had received a bicycle earlier, and he and I made many, many trips that spring and summer of about fifteen miles each way back to Grandma's for a good meal. When we weren't working, we were on the bicycle going just about everywhere. Grandma's good meals were the biggest attraction to us most of the time.

Late that summer I went back to Papa's more determined than ever to find something better, that, I hoped, would be the Army. My Uncle Tommy and my brother Jim joined the Army in 1936 and 37. By my comparison and my reasoning they were living high on the hog, I desperately wanted some of it. I was sure hoping and planning that it would be the Army. The problem was that

I was only fourteen and would have a few impatient years to wait. Unless I found a way to get in the Army on my own I would have to farm. Besides Grandma did not want me to get into the Army, I would not get much help from her. As I think of the past I also realize that I had a closeness with family that enabled me to survive these and other ordeals. A special feeling during these times for family made it all possible. I cherish memories of back then. We had many wonderful good times; it wasn't all bad. It was also the beginning of my eyes being opened to another world. One of good food, good clothes, and a little money. My Uncle Tommy and Jim had all these goodies, plus a motorcycle and later a car. They came home pretty often and let me go with them some. On one of these outings Jim bought me a hamburger, my first one ever, it looked about as big as a watermelon and it was just as good.

In the summer of 1939 a great experience was when Jim took me for a week or so to Fort Benning Georgia where he was stationed. Jim was an MP and we ate at the Post Stockade Mess. The stockade was enclosed by a high fence. Everyone going in was more or less searched. Of course I was all eyes for all these new things and loved the chow. I slept in the barracks in Jim's bed and he slept in a buddy's bed that would be on duty. I made out just fine except at times when the officers came around. Then I stayed out of sight. This was quite an experience and education for a country boy, good or bad I loved every minute. As a result, I started planning on how to get into the Army, and the sooner the better.

When I turned fifteen in September 1939, I went to Pensacola, Fla., to join into the Army. I told the Army people at Fort Brancas that I was eighteen and ready to serve. They told me that I needed my parents or guardian's permission to enlist, and that I did not have. They were very nice, sympathetic but amazed that a fuzzy faced kid wanted to get into the Army. Of course they didn't enlist me and I was very disappointed.

After leaving the Army post and returning to Pensacola it was too late to start back home; it was fifty miles to walk or ride, (ride if you were lucky at hitch hiking). I don't remember eating in town but I am almost sure that they fed me before I left the Army base that evening. I do remember that I did not have any money. I settled down on a bench placed along the wide main street in Pensacola. About nine or ten that night a policeman came by and checked me out. After getting the details of why I was there he took me to police headquarters for the night; saying that he did not want me sleeping on the streets. I didn't know much about the police, or what their job was, and I was rather puzzled and worried as to what would happen. It was a nice feeling when I realized that they were concerned about me, particularly the next morning when they gave me something to eat and sent me on my way.

I had learned enough to plan another try. Try again I did in January 1940. I got my Uncle to sign papers that I was eighteen, and he were my guardian, and that I had his permission to enter the Army. I didn't have Grandma's permission though. This time I went to Mobile, Alabama, being afraid that I would be recognized in Pensacola. Having to hitch hike and walk made it a very long trip; in fact it took all day, so I had to wait till the next morning for the recruiting office to open. I slept in a park that night and it was cold. The next day I took the written test and passed it. The test couldn't have been hard, for I just finished grammar school (six grades) and I certainly didn't know much. I don't remember much about the written test and the physical test wasn't much either; I could see, hear, and walk, that was about the extent of the physical. One did have to meet the weight and height requirements, I didn't weigh enough. I don't remember exactly how much I weighed but I was supposed to weigh at least one hundred and thirty-eight pounds. I lacked three pounds or so of weighing enough to get into the Army. The sergeant told me that if I would eat as many bananas as I could, I might make it. Mobile was a banana port, and bananas cost next to nothing, maybe ten cents a dozen. I think I started with a nickels worth (half dozen). Anyway, I didn't eat enough. I was still under weight and would have to get a waiver to get into the Army. The necessary paperwork for the waiver was filled out and I was told that I would hear something later. I thought that was the end of this try and that I had failed again. I had not made any plans about not being accepted.

I was heart broken, and discouraged about not being able to become a soldier and maybe get some of the good things in life (food, clothes, and a dab of money). Grandma did not want me to get into the Army and predicted that the Army wouldn't take me. I was inclined to agree with her after this failure.

Fort Devens MA. summer 1941. It certainly wasn't much to gripe about for a young country boy that knew what hard times were. I was experiencing new sights, new people, Fort Devens, and New England were wonderful and a good place to soldier. I was a contented soldier and always tried to do my best. And for what I was awarded the follow during my career; Combat Infantryman's Badge, Silver Star, Bronze Star W/V device for valor, and Oak Leaf Cluster. Purple Heart, Army Commendation Medal with two Oak Leaf Clusters, Good Conduct Medal with five clasps, American Defense Service Medal, American Campaign Medal, European Middle East Theater Medal with seven campaign stars and arrowhead for three invasions, World War II Victory Medal, Army of Occupation Medal (Japan), National Defense Service Medal, Korean Service Medal with four campaign stars, and the United Nations Service Medal. Foreign awards are the French Fourragere, and the Korean Presidential Citation. All received because most always I was serving with good soldiers, and was in the right place at the right time.

CHAPTER THREE
New Life and Creating
A Doughboy

Back home I got into the routine of farming, cutting stalks and breaking ground for the new crop. A few weeks later, to my surprise, I received a letter waiving the weight requirement and advising me that I would be allowed to enter the Army. I could not believe it and I wasted no time getting back to Mobile. Then, on to Montgomery where I was sworn in on 16 February 1940, as a soldier of the United States Army. Oh what a day! I was overjoyed. The Army had a fifteen-year old apprehensive apprentice; five foot eleven inch, one hundred thirty five-pound farm boy; lacking very much in knowledge, but determined to do his best. The recruiting sergeant drove (the four of us, three other men had just joined the Army) to the train station and put us on the train; destination Ft. Benning, Ga., and the First Infantry Division. This was my introduction to the Army's game of hurry up and wait. We waited, waited, and waited; and again we waited some more. I finally got off the train and went into the train station where much was happening. To a country boy it captured my attention. After thirty minutes or so I leisurely strolled back to the platform to where the train was supposed to be and there was no train. As I looked down the track I saw it slowly departing. I just could not escape the horror of being AWOL on my first day in the Army. This experience taught me that one can do just about anything if they want to badly enough. I felt that I ran as fast as I wanted to, and I barely caught the train. I had learned that you don't goof around in the Army.

We arrived at Ft. Benning late that night and I wasn't impressed with the Army's chow the first day in the Army. We were late for the regular meal and didn't get anything to eat. We had only one meal that day. However it did improve, starting the next day. I received blankets and a bunk in a large warehouse and waited for clothing and assignment to various First Division Units that were camped in the Harmony Church area. The next day we went to get clothing. They couldn't fit me, everything too baggy except shoes, socks, and underwear, the first underwear I had ever owned. My sizes were not on hand, such as, 27or28X33 trousers and 36or37L jacket. It would be a couple of weeks before I received my uniforms.

A couple of days later I was assigned to "E" Company, 26th Infantry Regiment, where I remained till 1945. Having no uniforms, I did not start recruit training for a week or so but it was not dull for they had plenty of other things for me to do. I policed the area, dug stumps, dug and cleaned latrines, dug kitchen sumps, worked in the kitchen (KP), and whatever else they could think of. To top it all off February 1940 was the coldest winter month at Fort Benning that there had been in years. So, without all the digging and other work, I don't think I would have made it through that cold Georgia winter with my skimpy clothing. Company "E" was billeted in tents and next to us was the PX, also in a large tent. It was my job to be the gofer for our tent. My bunk mates were all old soldiers and, the beer drinkers; they would send me for the beer. I did not join in the beer drinking. The reason they sent me was that in order to leave the Company area in the evenings one had to be in uniform or appropriate civilian clothes and they didn't want to dress up. So here the pecking order was used, or the totem pole, and I was at the bottom (so I was the gofer). In a week or so I received my basic issue of clothing and an M-1 rifle and recruit training began. The Army has a lot of pride in taking youngsters, such as me, and making soldiers out of them. The saying in the Army is that soldiers are made, not born. I will have to agree with that after the training of about nineteen recruits in my group. I must say, the Army was very successful in making soldiers of us. I also began to learn some facts of life that were different from what I had learned on the farm in south Alabama, living in a Hardshell (Primitive) Baptist environment. Down on the farm you believed and trusted your friends and neighbors. I learned very quickly that some people would take advantage and use you when they could. I learned that there are a few perverts in this world that I had been cautioned about. We new Doughboys stuck together and it presented no problem. I paid attention and learned whom I could trust and built many lasting friendships.

The majority of the men in Company "E" 26th were from the north and we recruits were southerners. There were about nineteen of us that were assigned to the unit at Ft. Benning; seven from Tennessee, two Alabamians, two Georgians, one Mississippian, two North Carolinians, two Oklahomans, and two from Texas. You can bet on it when I say that we stuck together like glue for a purpose. We were a close knit group and became very good friends and buddies; I mean the best ever. We took care of each other.

Recruit training in 1940 was a serious business, if you didn't hear or understand everything that was demonstrated you were in big trouble. In other words deep s... I had my moments of dumbness, but it didn't take me long to learn; especially having to pay for goofing by having to run a half mile or so, or by doing twenty or fifty push ups. Even dug a few pine tree stumps. This makes one pay attention. I would be exhausted after some of these pay attention punishments. I was completely burned out; my knees like rubber and trembling, very apprehensive and a bit scared but never did I regret joining the Army. Many times with anxieties, anger, fear, and hard spots, I was always 100% Army. After my basic training and making sharpshooter with the M-1 rifle, I was assigned to a rifle platoon as the platoon runner. On my first field problem our platoon set up positions and I was sent to the Company Command Post (CP) to let them know that we were in position and so forth. The first Sergeant sent me right back to the platoon with information as to chow, etc. When I got back to the platoon, I was pooped, so out of breath that I could hardly talk. The platoon leader asked me why I was out of breath, I told him that I ran to the CP and back. I was asked then why I had ran, I was very serious when I said, "I am a runner ain't I?" They cracked up and then explained that I did not have to run all the time.

Next was a Motor March that lasted almost two weeks. A motor march is a brain exercise for officers, moving troops, equipment, and vehicles with expertise, through South Georgia, Panhandle of Florida, and back to Fort Benning. At our first campsite the First Sergeant, (Bonehead) Harrison was calling out names for details; these details were to erect tents, dig latrines, kitchen sumps, and whatever. He came to a name he had trouble pronouncing. It went something like this; "Ko-lee," "Ka-ole," "Key-hole," no answers. Then he spelled it out, "Koehl." A very meek voice answered, "Here Sergeant, you pronounce that Cole." The First Sergeant stood about a foot taller and said, "I don't give a GD how you pronounce it, when I howler, Keyhole, Asshole, you answer!" Back in those days Enlisted Men were not noted for being well educated. Bonehead Harrison was a WW1 Veteran, big, crude, rough, tough, and mean (about like Hager the Viking), and, a very good soldier. Because of a WW1 wound he had a steel plate in his head, when he could not hear us, we called him Bonehead. This trip to Florida was really a fun trip for us. We did no training except Retreat and weapons inspection. We would play on the beach and scrounge around.

Being new in a company of Yanks and being the butt of their jokes and ridicule, we fellows from the south were determined to prove that we could be good soldiers. I think we did prove it, for by the time we landed in Oran, North Africa, there were ten or so in this bunch of southerners left, and in combat there were two Distinguished Service Cross winners, many Silver Stars, and Bronze Stars, Purple Hearts, and five Killed in Action. All of us became NCO's, and one received a field commission. The Army is the first to say that NCO's are the backbone of the Army and I do believe we were good and did what we were trained to do.

During the training of 1940, 41 and 42 we trained extensively, having a lot of fun along the way while training day and night, maneuvers in Louisiana-Texas, upper New York, North Carolina, including much amphibious training all very hard. We were young, we were tough, we were lean and mean (me, just plain skinny). And we were told that we were good and would become better. It is worth repeating that we as southerners, were at first ridiculed, made fun of, insulted, you name it, we experienced it all. There were a few squabbles, nothing serious, nor anything settled; we just soldiered that much harder. We had heritage, traditions, pride, and we learned quickly.

When on field problems the kitchen was equipped with cast iron coal/wood cooking stoves and the biggest job ever was keeping the stoves hot enough to cook. I don't have to tell you who had to do that job but I will, the new men. Plus we dug sumps, latrines, erected tents for the CP and kitchen. And to top it all the officers had to be pampered, get their tents and bunks set up. We peons had to clean up after them, plus. I suppose this was when I sorta started disliking officers. There was much difference in comfort furnished to officers and enlisted men. They were pampered with tents, bunks, tables and chairs, best of the chow, plus we were the dog robbers. This difference slowly narrowed in the Infantry in combat. I considered most were just a pain and a bunch of prima donnas. I have also known some of the best ever.

After recruit training we stayed in the field until we left for the Louisiana-Texas Maneuvers of 1940. The trip from Ft. Benning was a typical Army move, traveling about a hundred or so miles a day by truck. From a sight seeing view point it was great; I had just barely been out of the State of Alabama and every place I went was new to me. On this short trip we camped at Meridian and Vicksburg, Mississippi, Monroe, Louisiana and on the banks of the Sabine River, then we started playing war for a few weeks. It was an exhausting and hot few weeks. About everyone smoked and ready rolls were used for the first of the month smoking and as the money got low we smoked Bull Durham and such. While on maneuvers in Lousisiana I learned that you shouldn't store things in your gas mask. We carried gas masks on all field problems and the Louisiana maneuvers lasted for many weeks and of course the

PX was not with us in the field and we stocked up on Bull Durham or anything we could afford. This was also the era before plastic and a big problem for us was to keep things dry. I had bought a supply of Bull Durham and put it in my gas mask. We were making an assault on a hot humid morning and we had a simulated gas attack. That meant we had to put on our gas masks. So I had to rearrange my sacks of Bull Durham. Finally getting my gas mask on I started running again, up the hill. I was hot, I was sweating, and had to breathe very hard to get enough air. Breathing tobacco and tobacco fumes with the air I soon began to feel faint and just plain sick. It was not long before I began to up-chuck. The more I vomited the sicker I got. There was some concern about my condition, maybe a heat stroke, heat exhaustion, plus other guesses. Noncommissioned Officers and Officers were not supposed to let this happen to their men; and, it was more or less their butt they were worried about. You can bet that I wasn't about to tell them the reason I was sick, but it didn't take long for me to get better. Needless to say that was the last time I stored things in my mask. Finally the Louisiana-Texas maneuvers were over and we made camp in pup tents for a short while to clean up a bit before taking off for Ft. Devens, Massachusetts by motor convoy.

It was quite a trip, with overnight camps in Vicksburg, Mississippi, Birmingham, Alabama, Cleveland, Tennessee, Staunton, Virginia and such all the way to Ft. Devens, Massachusetts. Repeating, I had never been anyplace, so every place we went and things were new to me, I will always remember it. Even though I remember the trip fairly well it is hard for me to elaborate on the joy I experienced on this trip. Seeing so much that I had never seen, meeting people of different nationalities, unusual foods, and miles and miles of countryside very different from South Alabama. This was a trip of a life time for a country boy and it was compared to trips of later years. It took us about twelve days to make the trip and the people along the way made us very welcome. Arriving at Fort Devens Massachusetts in June was another exciting experience. We were billeted in brick barracks, which was a large step up after almost six months in the field. Not being used to modern baths and kitchens, bunks with sheets, recreation rooms, gym equipment and a firing range in the attic or basement, we were really living high on the hog. I did not go to town very often nor did I drink. I spent a lot of time just horsing around, trying to box or wrestle, and practice on the indoor firing range. We trained only in the morning and if we did not have a work detail in the afternoon we were on our own; in other words we goofed off.

Late summer and into fall we went to up state New York on maneuvers which was more or less a fun trip to me. Upper New York is really beautiful that time of the year and was great, cool nights and warm days. Our transport to New York and back to Ft. Devens was on rented civilian dump trucks, flat bed, stake bodies, trucks of every shape and size. It was a ragged looking convoy by Army standards. We were to play enemy for National Guard troops. Some of them used sticks for rifles, and stove pipes for mortars. That was a lot of substituting! We were also placed on a road as guards as President Roosevelt drove slowly by while on one of his campaign trips of 1940 and he visited troops in that area.

Returning to Ft. Devens the Second Battalion moved into the new, modern brick barracks completed while we were on maneuvers in New York. Now this was really uptown living. It did not take us long to get back into the routine of garrison life, half day duty/work schedule. A few weeks after we returned, I was detailed to be the Battalion fireman. The system provided hot water and heat for the new barracks. The most modern equipment, everything was automatic except for cleaning and removing ashes once every twenty four hours. We had coal for fuel and the cleanup was a big, big job. The boiler room had to be spotless, but still I had a lot of free time. After about six weeks it became dull and I had enough of the goofing off. I liked most all of the training the Company was doing at this time, particularly the training at night. It was fun to mess around, just play and hide in the snow. The Army tried very hard to make a soldier out of me, instead the horsing around in the snow brought the boy out in me.

Late 1940 and early 41 we began to build up to full strength and we received a lot of men from New England. We mingled very well and many lasting friendships developed. All of us who entered the unit at Ft. Benning, Feb. 1940, were still considered recruits by the old timers. So these new men from New England and us southerners stuck together for mutual benefits. In sticking together we hoped we might get some slack from the old timers. Soon they began sending the old soldiers out to form new units and train new men and sectional rivalry began to fade as we had too many other things to think about.

Training began to pick up at a fast pace in 1941. About the end of February after many months of over and over training on the 60mm mortar the Brass directed that all men in the mortar sections take the gunners qualification test. So on a very cold morning with the ground frozen as hard as concrete they gave the tests. In my company I was the first to take the test and barely passed, I scored just a passing seventy-one. In the training exercises I had always scored very high. I was very disappointed and somewhat embarrassed. I was considered one of the best gunners in the company. After all the testing was completed for the regiment, only two had passed. I was one, not bad for a sixteen year old farm boy from South Alabama. Amphibious training starting in the spring forty-one and then every year through 1944; with the largest ever in June 1944 which was no dry run, plus Oran and Sicily. Amphibious training teaches the art of making assaults on hostile beaches from small boats, day or night. First there were a few weeks at Buzzard Bay, Massachusetts on an old Army transport ship, the USS Kent.

(THERE WILL BE NUMEROUS COMMENTS BY RODNEY H. L'AMOURUEX. THEY WILL BE BRACKETED, AND IDENTIFIED BY THE INITIALS, RHL). (RHL. Prior to the regiment leaving Fort Devens for Cape Cod a small cadre of our own men was selected to go in advance to be taught, by the Coast Guard, how to operate the landing craft. The idea being that if, in the real thing, the Navy helmsman operating the boat got killed or wounded on the way to the beach there would be an Army man on board who could at least get the craft onto the beach. When the regiment arrived on the USS Kent and started landing exercises many were surprised to see their own buddies operating the landing craft. And I am sure some had doubts that the small boats would ever get to the designated landing areas).

Amphibious training was new to us and we soon found out it was also very hard work. It sapped the strength right out of you; climbing up or descending cargo nets, getting seasick (for many it is dreadful), getting saltwater wet, having sand all over you and into everything, running in the sand and over the sand dunes all will make you rubber kneed. It doesn't take long to get a belly full. The most irritating of all these was the saltwater and sand. Any place on one's body that is rubbed by rifle belts, packs, is raw, burning, hurting, and very miserable. You get wet, then sand gets into everything, there is nothing but saltwater showers later on the ship. I had never taken a saltwater shower and felt clean. To me a saltwater shower is worse than not taking one at all. Many were prone to become seasick, accordingly what I've been told that is the worst thing that could happen to a person. Some would get sick as soon as their feet hit the gang plank. Lucky me, I was never seasick and I had fun telling the sick ones it was just in their head. At times they wanted to shoot me (when and if they recovered).

On another training exercise several weeks later we sailed from New York to the North Carolina coast on the USS Leonard Wood. Summer of 1943 we took the sister ship to the Leonard Wood from Oran, Algeria to Algiers, on one of our amphibious training exercises. I don't recall the name of that ship; we heard that it was sunk in the Pacific. We were lucky to be on the Leonard Wood for one of the boilers burned out and we docked in Charleston, SC for a week or so. We had a Company party at the St. Frances Hotel which was an up town hotel in its day. It was a welcome break from the ship's food, and the suffocating heat on the ship. (No air conditioning in the forties).

Amphibious training is very hazardous, strenuous and exhausting and offers a double dose for people that are prone to sea sickness. When making a landing every day, you don't have much time for loafing. Starting early in the morning at three-four a.m. loading onto the LCIA (Landing Craft Infantry Assault) in darkness and then spend a few hours wallowing around on the rough water, giving those who felt sick plenty of time to get sicker. Then its full speed to the beach. An LCIA, LCI (Landing Craft Infantry), and LCVP (Landing Craft Vehicle-personnel) carry about thirty or forty men and just about everyone has a different name for these boats. Some don't know the difference. A few hours on land taking the assigned objectives and then its load onto the LCIA and back to the ship. Then eat, clean weapons, try to get the sand and rust off your weapons, and out of your clothing, and spend the rest of the day on this chore. It is not an easy operation. I might note that land lubbers learn a lot on amphibious operations; such as, that one can do their laundry at sea. Just take a rope and fasten your cloths on it, and throw them in the water and the sea will do the washing; but, if you forget them, when you pull the rope in all you have left is a knot. In the fall of '41 there were maneuvers again in North Carolina, around Ft. Bragg. A lot of moving, a lot of traveling and much for a country boy to see, I never got tired of looking, and many, many new experiences. We knew what we were training for, combat, and we knew it would eventually come. Training was very tough and exhausting, but in a short period of time I would recover and be ready to have another go at it.

When we had time off we lived life to its very fullest, I was no longer the naive country boy, thanks to Elmer Miller and a few others. When the maneuvers were over I asked and got a ten-day leave before the Company left North Carolina for Ft. Devens. I had just arrived home at Atmore, Alabama when all hell broke loose in the Pacific, the start of WW11 for us. My leave was cut short and I started back to Ft. Devens. Everything was somewhat unsettled, not knowing what to expect. The Companies were assigned special guard duties and were being placed at water systems, warehouses and such. My detail guarded the pumping stations, storage tanks and wells that were the water system for the town of Ayer and all of Ft. Devens. There was one Officer of the Guard, or Officer of The Day, who would park his vehicle some distance away and walk to our guard post, trying to catch us smoking or goofing off. Needless to say, we didn't like such tactics. It got more or less predictable as to what he would do. We couldn't relax, (really we weren't supposed to) and we had to watch for him. We did not like being checked on in this manner. So my good friend and buddy Frazier made plans to try to stop the sneaking around. We were guarding the warehouses one night when we decided to try out our plan. We watched for him and finally he parked his car

A Doughboys Narrative •

and turned off the lights. Frazier got behind the warehouse on the railroad tracks and I was in front on the street. The Officer of the Guard (or Day) started sneaking down the side of the railroad tracks, Frazier waited until the OD was close enough to challenge, then Frazier fired off a shot over his head and yelled, "Halt!" The OD started yelling, identifying himself, Frazier told him to "Advance and be recognized." He started in on Frazier, chewing him out, and wanted to know why he shot before challenging. Frazier replied, "I did challenge but the Lieutenant didn't stop, Sir." By this time I had gotten around to where they were and I backed Frazier up by saying,"I heard Frazier challenge the Lieutenant, Sir." After that the OD made sure that he made enough noise for us to hear him coming. There was no sneaking after that night.

After a month or so things became normal again and training started at a more furious pace. January-February 1942 and another amphibious exercise began. We boarded the ship in New York and sailed for Virginia Beach, VA. It was a miserable operation with snow on the beach and we used the old type landing craft without ramps. We had to go over the sides of the landing craft and got completely wet, plus having to wade in a few feet of water to the beach for some distance. Oh how miserable life can be!

Returning to Ft. Devens we started packing for Camp Blanding, FL. We were sad about leaving Ft. Devens, it had been our home for about a year and a half. At Fort Devens the National High School Band competition and the National Rifle competition at Wakefield were held. The Army hosted these major events and it was a great treat. Plus a couple of open house get acquainted events to the public, that were big hits. A lot of firing squad details and many small parades to celebrate various events in small towns in New England. On these short trips we would have a rifle rack to secure our weapons so that they could be taken back to Ft. Devens, and then most of us would stay and participate in the celebrating. Plenty of good food, good wholesome fraternizing, and girls, girls, girls. We met a lot of people and were treated very well indeed. We loved Ft. Devens and New England. In 1941 (I believe) there were a lot of forest fires in New England, and we fought many of these fires which helped to build up a good relationship with the New Englanders.

After much joking about going to Florida for a winter vacation we soon found out that the making of a soldier must go on and the training turned out to be the most extensive we had encountered. Day and night, day after day, on and on; physical fitness, weapons training, forced marches, and lots and lots of night training. Included in our training was many runs repeatedly on the obstacle course. We ran the course in two men teams. Mock, was the strength of the team and I was the agile part of the team. Believe it or not, Mock and I were the champs, with a very high score. By no means was it a vacation. We were continually on the go stumbling around in the woods, or brush and the low areas (swamps) where there were cypress trees with lots of cypress knees, little stumps. It was not an easy task. I did not learn the correct name for the cypress [knees] until many years later. My son went through Ranger school and trained in Florida for a few weeks. When he came home, he mentioned something about the damnit stumps in Florida. I, being sort of curious and thought I knew a little about Florida asked, "What in the hell is a damnit stump?" He replied, "fumbling around in the dark, on an exercise, guys would stumble on a cypress knee and fall on a cypress knee which hits you in the chest or belly. Then you would hear a thump, a grunt and, damnit!" We had a small amount of fun while at Camp Blanding but mostly training and more training, just hell. I left camp only twice while there, that indicates how busy we were. I think it was May we were told that we would be moving. As to when, where, or for what, we weren't told.

(RHL. Rumors started to fly as to where the outfit might be going next, and some who believed that our next departure would take us overseas really went all out and shaved their heads. As it was proven later this was a little premature so the ones who had to go around bald received a lot of kidding from the others).

The end of May we went to Ft. Benning for more training, joint armor, air, and infantry exercise. Of course a bit more training with heat, dust and running, just trying to stay with the tanks day after day was a bit more hell. My brother Jim participated in the same exercise. He was a tank platoon Sgt. and tank commander. We visited in the evenings and drank a little hot beer. They would bring us beer by the truck loads; the more they brought to us, the more we drank. They never caught up, we bought it all. I didn't care much for beer, and particularly this we were getting was green [not aged], hot, and second rate. We drank it because there was none around any better. One thing it would do is give one of the worst hangovers that you would ever have.

June we went to Indiantown Gap, Pennsylvania, our staging Post for overseas shipment. We trained some but not as much as we did at Blanding and Ft. Benning. We fired on the range zeroing our weapons and after that we usually had the afternoons off. Indiantown Gap was a fun place, the people were the best ever, friendly, accommodating, and they did everything possible to make our short stay memorable. They knew that we were on our way overseas with many unknowns. For my buddies and me the fun place was Pottsville. There was a Polish Polka club there and on Fridays and Saturdays the place was jumping. Friday nights was pot luck supper night. We were told not to bring anything to eat, just help them eat. Friendships were instantaneous; they took to us and us to them; food, beer, and girls. It was hard for us to spend our money there. It would have been great if I could have remembered some of these people and visited them in later years. I will always regret not keeping in touch.

(RHL. There was also a great USO Club at Lebanon which was close to the post. Many soldiers spent time there at dances and other activities. Indiantown Gap was the one place that we had been stationed where the non-commissioned officers were allowed to live off the post. Quite a few took advantage of this and had their wives join them for the last few weeks before they shipped out. Then one day there was quite a scene at the Lebanon train station as the train cars rolled slowly by loaded with soldiers. Some bald, leaning out of the windows waving goodbye to their wives and the people of Lebanon).

Prior to departure we had packed our duffel bags and back packs, nothing extra just the essentials. In time we didn't even have much of that left. Move after move we had been discarding our personal possessions until we didn't have anything but a tooth brush, a spoon, and maybe an extra pair of socks. The Army started stripping us of our goodies and extra stuff when we left Ft. Devens for Camp Blanding. We left Indiantown Gap with only our scant basic issue, no civilian clothes, no extra uniforms, or anything else. By the time we made the invasion of North Africa all we had, had been on our backs. As I think back to south Alabama, on the farm, all we had was good neighbors, love, hard work, and to most honesty. It's hard for me to say what we had on down the road in Tunisia, Sicily, France, and into Germany. In order of importance I would say, determination, the will to survive, confidence, pride, a mean streak I suppose, and love for our buddies, and, perhaps a few unmentionables.

That afternoon we walked down to the train station at Indiantown Gap. Late that afternoon we boarded the train for Hoboken N.J., and then a ferry ride to board HMS Queen Mary. I believe it was berthed at pier 91.

A Doughboys Narrative •

CHAPTER FOUR
Retrospect, Com-Se Com-Sae

I think that maybe I should elaborate a little about the life of a DOUGHBOY (Me) in the early years of my Army life. What I did for past time, hobbies, habits, recreation, good or bad. For the first year or so of my Army service I was on the goody goody side of what was normal for most soldiers. When I was off duty, it was a little boxing, physical fitness, and hand to hand combat. We had equipment for all of these activities, plus target practice in the basement or attic of our barracks. I never reached the status of an expert in any of these activities. The Post Theater was just across the street and I probably saw every movie shown there. In winter nearby there was a good place to skate on the Post. I purchased a good pair of skates and after many painful falls I became a pretty good skater.

In the fall of 1941 I began going out with my buddies on payday, we would have good meal, drink a bit, and just horse around, nothing really bad. Of course this could be a matter of opinion I suppose. When we went to Wake-field, Massachusetts, I would go with Elmer Miller "look-ing" around and he was responsible for opening my eyes too many facts of life. Miller was from Johnson City, Ten-nessee and was one of my best friends ever. He was sorta mean and mischievous; yet a fun type of guy, very likea-ble, and very, very tough, rather fight than to eat, and I was the coat holder. Before getting into the Army Miller associated with a very rough bunch. I never saw anyone who tangled with Miller that didn't get their plow cleaned. Miller carried a knife and when a "queer" approached him or us, he would grab his tie, cut it off, stick it in their face and say, "if I see you again this will be your tongue." In some of the rough places we visited he was better than insurance.

Hardly ever did we go out on the town without meet-ing a girl or two; we knew a few in most of the towns around Ft. Devens. Miller didn't like drinking much, nor did I so we went to the movies, had a coke or a bite to eat afterwards; and this was more or less an evening out with the girls for us. The girls I met were about the same age as I was, sixteen/seventeen and would not be served in a bar anyway. I went out solo mostly when I had a steady. I had a couple of very special friends and have regretted not keeping in touch when we left Ft. Devens and Indi-antown Gap. I met a very special girl the first weekend after we arrived at Indiantown Gap and went with her until the day we left for Europe. The people from all around came out to welcome us the first weekend at Indiantown Gap. This girl was one of the welcoming crowd, we met and we were special to each other. This girl and a couple of others at Ft. Devens tried to keep in touch with me. In my predicament I saw no reason to do so with such an uncertain future. Right or wrong I be-lieved, to be out of sight was out of mind and that was the best way to end a relationship. There are feelings either way and it really makes no difference how you break off.

Ft. Devens was a good place to train in 1940 and '41, small compared to other Army Posts, there wasn't much harassment nor "grabbass" going on. Everyone did their job and got along well. Our hikes were taken on the back roads and trails through apple orchards and small farms. It was a standing order that we were not to pick apples, not even off the ground. On one of our hikes we were going through an apple orchard and one of the fellows picked one. The next day he was a Private, it was certain that an order back then meant exactly what it said and if anyone disobeyed an order they suffered the consequences. I have mentioned before of our participation in ceremonies, celebrations and honor guard details in areas around New England. We were detailed to these events and at times some of the men selected to go would have other plans. It was permitted to get someone to take your place and many times that someone would be me. I would go every chance given to me. The people were very congenial, doing everything possible to make us welcome and feel at home. Plus there were girls and a few dollars if you had taken someone's place.

The Army maneuvers in the fall of 1940 in up state New York was one of the most enjoyable operations that I ever participated in. We were the enemy for the New York and New England National Guard. We did not have to do any hiking, just set up a defense and then they would attack. When we were in these positions the local people would bring us all sorts of good things to eat, even hot coffee in the early morning hours. The civilians were beginning to accept the military and went out of their way to do things for us. It is wonderful to feel that you are appreciated. The weather was just right, warm sunny days and comfortable nights. It seemed as if the Army was getting better each day, especially while on maneuvers in

New York. To me every day in the Army was like Sunday on the farm.

I just don't know exactly how to relate these stories or characterize them, so you can be the judge. These stories are two of the many that I could tell. One must realize we were being programmed to kill and the mean dirty things we learned and did, did not seem to bother us. In a way it was, hurrah for me (and your buddies) and to hell with everyone else. We considered this a fact of life. On payday about six of us, occasionally more would start with a steak dinner at the Hotel Ayer, followed by a night on the town. Most always we would go to Worcester hitting the high spots until the late hours. Which meant that we would have to get a cab back to Ft. Devens. If not a cab we would catch the morning milk train that stopped at about every farm between Worcester and Ayer. It was generally thirty minutes or an hour behind time and we did not like taking a chance of being late for reveille. But this particular payday we took a cab back. The new shiny pennies had just been put into circulation. When we arrived at the barracks Cunliffe yelled, "I'll pay it," and he did, with shinny new pennies counted as dimes. To us GI's it was great, we had finally stuck a cab driver. In those days cab drivers weren't our favorite people. You might wonder why anyone would have that many pennies with them. We carried them for defense; as it doesn't take but one punch with a roll of pennies in your fist and most always the advantage was yours.

I did not plan to tell of this little incident, but I will. We were on a roll one night and after a few hours of boozing it was decided that we would go to a house of ill repute that someone had told us about. After much laughing and whooping it up we found the place. And we went inside still very noisy so that everyone knew we were in the neighborhood. Before things got started the Police raided the joint. The Police marched all of us GI's out of the house with a few threats and preceded to arrest all the women. The "ladies" denied doing anything wrong, which they had not while we were there. Things got a bit confusing when one of the fellows told the police we had given the girls money. Then one Policemen came out and asked, "What in the hell's been going on here; the women are saying they didn't do anything." I answered, "Maybe they didn't, but we paid them two dollars a piece, and we didn't do anything either, so we want our money back." To keep the Police from arresting them, the "ladies" gave us two dollars each. With this episode and the shiny pennies counting as dimes to pay our cab fare, I thought that we were on a big, big roll. I suppose one could say that we were sorta rowdy and would do most anything, but our consciences didn't bother us.

As I think back it is hard to believe that a sixteen year old country boy would have the smarts to do something like the following incident. While at Devens I was a prisoner chaser and given three general prisoners [men court martialed by a general court and sentenced to a few years] to clean the Officers Club. While cleaning the officers club one morning the prisoners would try to go in different directions, knowing full well that they were not to separate. The officers club was about a mile from the stockade and at noon as we started to return I gave the command, "Double time, march!" Making the prisoners double time all the way back to the stockade as I walked, giving them the command, "To the rear, march!", over and over. By the time we got to the stockade the Provost Officer had received a number of calls from Post Headquarters, and others, indignantly wanting to know what in the hell was going on. The Provost Sergeant rushed out of the guardhouse to find out. After halting my prisoners I explained to the Provost Sergeant what happened. He smiled and said, "Carry on." It was a standing order that a prisoner chaser took care of his prisoners. He took the necessary action to control his prisoners. You couldn't abuse them but disciplining them was permitted. I must have had a good explanation because I received compliments for my handling of the situation from the Provost Officer and Company Officers.

I have always been sorta proud of the outcome too. A few months later I was promoted to Corporal.

I have been sorta beating around the bush so to speak about some of the places I visited in the early forties. I have many very vivid pictures. I cannot get the proper words together to describe them. I will try to give some sort of an evaluation of these areas as I saw them. The small towns in Florida that HAD a pronounced Spanish influence were very impressively beautiful. Now, most are tinsel towns and depressive. I do not have any desire to visit some of the coastal areas, except maybe the Western Panhandle, and St. Augustine. In fact from New Jersey through Texas along the coast and the Coastal Plains, other than a few cities, just don't push my button. Some of the man made sights, museums and such, in the cities like Washington, D.C. Charleston and Savannah, and a dab of Philadelphia has much to offer the tourist. The mountain areas of Alabama/Georgia north through New England and Upper New York have much to see with unlimited beautiful scenery. I would never get tired of touring these areas. Some of the most vivid pictures are New Hampshire, Vermont, and upper New York. I could not do justice trying to describe these wonderful places. I will say, see them for yourself and you won't be disappointed. The most interesting cities to me are, Washington, D.C. Boston, New York, Atlanta, little of Philadelphia, Charleston, Savannah, and St. Augustine. This is not an all inclusive list, (a list now, 1993 would be different) for there are untold numbers of beautiful small towns. There are many that I plan and hope to visit.

CHAPTER FIVE
Turmoil, Overseas, England & Scotland, and Combat

Friday, 31 July 1942 we finished packing and were off duty until noon the next day. I went to my girl friend's and spent the night. Saturday morning her parents drove us to Indiantown Gap and we departed with a somewhat cheerless goodby. It was impossible for me to express my feelings. My feelings were mixed and maybe for most everyone that was departing. We were going into many unknown situations and possibilities. All of us GIs thought we knew what it was all about; we thought we were tough, no feeling of emotion, no regrets, and yet, very apprehensive, still there was a certain amount of sadness. I am mixing this up with us, we, and I, but all were probably torn in different directions. We were having about the same apprehensions, wanting just to get it over. Yet we were not anxious to go into combat. Hopefully one thing we all were looking for was MAYBE a slow down in the continuous exhausting over and over training. Most people do not realize the amount of training that it takes to be just mediocre. We of the First Division knew that we were better than mediocre, being second to none, the best. We had to believe we were the best. With much training we had paid the price to achieve that distinction and with much pride. Would you believe that there was NEVER ANY SLOW DOWN in training. If anything, we trained much harder. We were leaving a very good life, and the best friends ever, for the unknown. Knowing also that many would not come back. There were many things and people we would never see again. This fact was very vivid to me when I returned in April of 1945, for things had changed and so had the people. I have said we trained for a mission and that was the priority placed in our (my) hearts.

We arrived at Hoboken, New Jersey late at night, went across the harbor and boarded HMS Queen Mary. There were two soldiers for every bunk and we divided into two groups. We would switch every twenty four hours from sleeping on deck to sleeping in a cabin, up or down, out or in, or wherever; very crowded and difficult to find a place to sit, stand, or sackout. Some of us slept in the life rafts stacked on deck or in the bath tubs on the lower decks. It all worked out well and we didn't lose any sleep. I found out later that the Queen Mary had rafts and life boats for only just a few thousand. We had life jackets and I suppose we felt secure but you can't last long in the waters of the North Atlantic. With approximately fifteen thousand Soldiers, the mess (the right name for a British ship), feeds two meals a day, with about an hour between the two menus, of breakfast and dinner/supper. About the same menus day after day, and it took 20-22 hours to feed everyone. Meal tickets were issued and I being sorta a chow hound, even though the chow was terrible, with extra meal tickets one could be picky. Some people soon as their foot hit the gang plank or the ship started moving, they got sea sick. I collected extra meal tickets from them and would rub it in a bit, by saying that I would eat for them. They did not want to even think about food, and I would get a shoe thrown at me. I'm not bragging when I say, I have been on many voyages and I have never been sea sick.

The night we will always remember, 1 August 1942, we boarded HMS Queen Mary and left New York City, from pier ninety-one, 2 August 1942 for Glasgow, Scotland. The Queen Mary crossed the Atlantic without an escort, maneuvering skillfully and making sharp turns every few minutes made the ship list many degrees. The British had it figured out that by making these turns a sub could not hit the Queen Mary. I wasn't completely convinced, but I suppose they were right for it was never hit. Arriving at Gourock late Saturday and as we debarked we were greeted by Scottish Ladies with, a "cheerio Yanks." We thought that the ladies talked funny. They served us tea and crumpets; you can image what our comments were about the tea, but not to the ladies. Most of us did not like pre-mixed hot tea with powdered milk and sugar. We were very partial to coffee. The Division went by train to Tidworth Barracks, not far from Salisbury England. We were anxious to see England and Scotland; at daybreak we got our first look. My fist impression was good, England and Scotland were LOVELY. We were learning ENGLISH very quickly.

While at Tidworth, we were issued some new equipment. It was always a job to clean the cosmoline (hard, sticky grease) off the mortars, machine guns and rifles with the normal cleaning things we usually used stateside. Now, compared to what we had stateside to what we had in Tidworth we were really roughing it big; and it got much worse down the road. In our spare time we played football. Wearing GI shoes while playing was very rough

and some got injured. The Brass ended the football playing for that reason. I went to town only once while in
England and that was to Salisbury. (RHL. Others went to
London and came back with many stories of their experiences in the black outs. Such as taxi cabs going by with
blue head lights; most difficult to see and dodge, and
ladies of the night all over, particular at Picadilly Circus,
both day and night, equally difficult to see at night and
dodge).

We did not do much training but mostly we were
trying to get accustomed to the country as everything was
very strange to us. September we left Tidworth for Inver-
ary, Northern Scotland for more amphibious and hand to
hand combat training. This brutal hand to hand combat
course was given by the British Commandos. We were
quartered in tin huts and on HMS Warwick Castle, that
was anchored fairly close to our camp. The training was
normal, very tough; cold and wet most of the time. Or all
the time is more like it. We stayed on the ship when
practicing landings as the Brass wanted to make sure that
we knew how to climb the cargo net ladders. Climbing
and descending the cargo nets with a combat load makes
one want to be someplace else; makes one rubber kneed,
and zaps the strength out of you. We saw the sun very
little; just half a day out of the few weeks we were there.

We also experienced some of the lousiest chow while
on the ship that I have ever encountered, or ever will, I
hope. To make matters worse our mess crew did not do
much better. At this time our rations were mostly British
issue, we did get coffee and a few other items of GI issue.
Anyway it seems that GI's are at their best when they have
something to gripe about. If it had not been for the generous portion of bread I think I would have starved. We
slept in hammocks while aboard the ship that was a new
experience for most. Also being so crowded that they
would hang hammocks over the mess tables after we ate;

(Mess, still a very fitting name). The Commandos taught us hand to hand, knife throwing, and some off hand shooting techniques. I eventually became average or maybe a little better with the trench knife and off hand with the carbine. Many years later I was teaching my son how to shoot and hit the target. He was having trouble with sighting his rifle. So I told him it was a matter of concentration and a consistent sight picture. I took his twenty-two and said, "All you have to do is concentrate, like this," I hit a can at about 10 yards off hand. He said, "Pop, you can't do that again!" I fired again, knocking another can off the log. That was much better than I usually shoot, but to leave him with a good impression, I never tried it again.

There was not much excitement in Scotland where we were, no pubs, no beer. To like Scotch or English beer you have to make up your mind that there is none other available, and NO GIRLS. (RHL. A few got passes to go to Glasgow and had stories to tell about the large dance hall with a floor that went up and down while people danced. Many cute Scotch lassies were there to dance with the G.Is. There was one unsuspecting soldier who tried to spend the food coupons given to him before he left camp, on some handkerchiefs to send home to his new bride. Much to the amusement of the Scottish saleslady).

About the only amusing thing was that in our Company there was a fellow who seemed to always do the unusual. As we were leaving to return to Glasgow he got drunk. No one knew where the booze came from. Some had to manhandle him, carrying and dragging him, while others had to carry his equipment. The Company Commander came to see what the raucous or noise was, and started chewing out this poor drunk. The fellow listened for a moment and then said, "Get the hell outa here and leave me alone, or I will kick your ass so hard that your shirt tail will go up your back like a window shade." Of course everyone cracked up over that one. I don't think he got any punishment, for by the next day we were on the ship and on our way to North Africa.

It was late October when we went to Glasgow and boarded HMS Monarch of Bermuda, a wonderful ship. Any other time we would have enjoyed the trip. The first squad, (my squad) had the best berth that I ever had on a transport. We were in a cabin on the upper deck and always before we were about as far down in the hole as one could get. We couldn't help but think of what was ahead and that took most of the joy out of our tourist mood. During peace time the Monarch of Bermuda was on the run between New York and Bermuda. The ship had a wide promenade deck that we used to keep in shape by walking. There was concern about staying fit, so the promenade deck was used a lot. We were not sure where we were going, but suspected North Africa as General Montgomery was in need of some help. One of the most intriguing mysteries of the War was the rumor. We would be sure that we knew where we were going and what we were to do, then the rumors would start. We would hear the most convincing, so-called official poop, of where, when and why, many so logical and very possible, so convincing that you believed a little, or all of it. Because most always it sounded so good and there was a lot of hope that it would be true. You would get to the point that you didn't know what to believe. I think it was intended to confuse the enemy. We were in a fairly large convoy and we would count ships every day trying to see if any were missing, because there were submarines around a few times trying to get us. Counting ships didn't work because from day to day the count went up or down we could usually see about thirty to forty of all sorts. About the 4th or 5th of November we went through the Straits of Gibraltar at night, more or less confirming North Africa as the destination. One of the most interesting times aboard ship is at the time land is sighted. (RHL. We could see the dark outline of the Rock of Gibraltar against the moonlit sky but no other lights, due to the black out. Then looking south the lights from Tangier in Spanish Morocco could be seen shining brightly). There are many EXPERTS that know where we are and where we are going. This time was no exception, some would say France, others Portugal, Spain, Africa, is where we are. And where we were going, were more speculations. Many were convincing. It wasn't but only a few that really knew where we were and where we were going. Us lowly GI's didn't know anything.

(RHL. We did get some strange orders about our appearance such as, "cut off those beards." Some of us had taken advantage of the many days of sailing around in circles in the Atlantic, while the huge battle fleet assembled from England and the States, to grow great looking beards. However, top brass decided that it would be better if it didn't look as if we were mimicking the Arabs, most of whom had beards. So much to our regret, off they came).

The next day we started to get the poop as to where we were going, the objectives, and what to expect (nobody really knew for sure). The landing place was to be Les Andalouses, a small resort town about 10-15 miles west of Oran, Algeria. There was no way to tell how we felt about the landing as we were new at the combat game, emotions were very mixed; nervous, sweaty, anxiety, maybe a little scary, dread, and of course there were always one or two hard nuts, heros, let me at'em types. An invasion is like having a one way ticket to someplace you desperately don't want to go.

In November of 1942 there were equipment shortages. Our assault group had to use an LCVP (Landing Craft Vehicle Personnel), larger than an LCIA (Landing Craft Infantry Assault), and it was next too impossible to get close to the beach at Andalouses because of offshore sand bars. (RHL. We were informed to expect some resistance from the Free French. Mainly in the form of artillery which was in fortification, overlooking Oran Harbor. We were also told that the invasion was backed up by a vast armada of warships. And also that His Royal Majesties Battleship RODNEY was offshore in our sector with the mission to knock out the artillery that was looking down our throats. While our landing craft circled in its rendezvous area we could hear the whiz of 14" shells going overhead which were fired from the unseen battleship. Then shortly, an explosion flash high on the hill overlooking Oran. One of our sound leaders was extremely proud of this because his name was Rodney also). Our craft didn't make it to the beach and as we got off the LCVP and started wading, the water got deeper. It was about 5-6 feet and over our heads when the swells or waves came in. We had to bob the best we could with all the weight we were carrying. Carrying extra rations and ammunition made it a bit tough. The short people had to be helped to make it. King who was in my squad, was a short fellow and the water was over his head. But with luck and many days of amphibious training we were able to reach the beach.

Plastic bags such as we now have in the 90s would have been worth their weight in gold on this landing. Just about everything we had got wet. However three packs of cigarettes in my helmet were the only things of mine that did not get wet (just damp around the edges). As always there were some unusual happenings. Like when a certain Officer threatened the Navy helmsman with; get this boat moving or I will." He had his fortyfive in his hand when he said that. We were way out on the first sand bar at that time. The officer had already made it very clear to get in closer, even if it meant losing the boat. We did get closer after the threat. The largest, most robust man in my squad, Schwartz, was so sick (he gulped too much salt water) that when we got on the beach other squad members had to carry his mortar ammo and his pack. There were a couple of runts in my squad and you can bet that Schwartz, (the Charles Atlas type) took much ribbing for a long time, but he also could dish it out.

We were shelled a few times, not very effective but it scared us something awful. We encountered no serious ground action to speak of. (RHL. As I have said, this was our first live action encounter and we were not familiar with the sounds of war. We all knew enough to dive for a gully when we heard artillery shells coming. Then after a nearby explosion some would stick their heads up to see where it had landed, only to hear the buzzing of bees all around. It didn't take long to learn that the bees were shrapnel fragments from the exploded shell flying in all directions. From here on we kept our heads down until the "bees" stopped buzzing).

One of the most disgusting things to happen to us as we were approaching a small town on our way to Cape Falcon. There were a lot of trenches on the outskirts of town and as the shelling started everyone ran for the trenches and dove in. The people of the town also used these trenches, not for protection but as an outhouse. What a filthy, stinking mess it was, and it made a lasting impression on us as far as Africa was concerned. We learned North Africa wasn't the number one tourist attraction. In fact it stunk. The GI's saying was, "If the world ever needed an enema, it would be inserted in North Africa." We also said the same thing about North Korea. During the invasion of North Africa we were in enough action to say that we were combat veterans. Luckily there were only a few casualties. One of the pleasant parts of the landing was finding a couple cases of Portuguese sardines at the French Fort. Of course we liberated the same.

After the Company mopped up at Cape Falcon we went back toward Oran and to the top of the mountain west of Oran, where we set up camp. There was much destruction on the mountain. The battleship HMS Rodney hit the place pretty hard trying to knock out the French coastal guns. There were also many dead horses and the stench was terrible. The Monarch of Bermuda, our troop ship got hit by coastal guns and went to Gibraltar for emergency repairs before unloading our support gear. All of our gear, supplies, and kitchen were on the ship therefore we lived on British compo rations consisting of ox tail stew, plum pudding, a mixture of pre-mixed leaf tea, sugar, and powdered milk, and a few C rations. Appetizing, huh? We missed our few extras and our kitchen.

Story time: We would trade with the natives (Arabs) for wine and most anything to eat. Late one evening my good friend Miller traded for three bottles of wine, he and I lost no time in disposing of the same, saving an eye opener. As the contents of the bottles lowered there was sediment and we would have to sip the wine through our teeth. After a while we began to feel pretty good and it took some effort to save a few sips for an eye opener the next morning. The crap we drank or the quantity always left its mark, sick as a dog or a busting headache and sometimes both. The next morning I sipped the wine through my teeth and poured the sediment out. The sediment was bugs and flies. We were sorta sick and yuckie, and vomiting, green vomit. Lesson umpteen, live and learn as things happen. Another lesson is that two shouldn't eat a gallon of sliced pineapple and drink the juice at one sitting. After our kitchen arrived Miller was on KP and he stole or rather liberated a gallon of sliced pineapple; he and I ate it all, and drank the juice. Experiencing instances such as these you will learn how to pick hair out of your teeth.

Finally our kitchen arrived around the first of December, we were getting tired of such crappy rations and were wanting something different. About the same time we moved to a valley west of Oran near an orange grove and railroad track. The orange grove was guarded by Arabs armed with shotguns. On the first attempt at swiping oranges they fired warning shots to discourage us. We used the railroad as concealment to creep up close to the guards who were in watch towers. Then we would stand up so that they could see us with our rifles and if they fired, we fired. We were not in the fire for effect mode at this time. Shotguns were no-match against our rifles so we got as many oranges as we wanted. The Brass didn't like our tactics and soon put a stop to it. Oran was dominated by the French for many years and some of their customs were very evident. One was cat houses. The first month or so everything was wide open, then the Army took over and posted places off limits, pro (prophylactic) stations, and the whole nine yards. All entrances were guarded and if one even went into this area you could not leave without taking a pro.

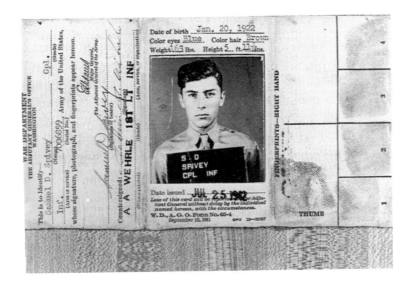

Date of birth Jan. 20, 1922
Color eyes Blue. Color hair Brown
Weight 163 lbs. Height 5 ft. 11 ins.

S D
SPIVEY
CPL INF

Date issued JUL 25 1942

Loss of this card will be reported to The Adjutant General without delay by the individual named hereon, with the circumstances.

W. D., A. G. O. Form No. 65-4.
September 10, 1941   GPO 16-22357

FINGERPRINTS—RIGHT HAND

4	3	2	1

THUMB

WAR DEPARTMENT

WASHINGTON, D. C.

Identification Card
No. O- 139940

CHAPTER SIX
Tunisia & Tough Lessons

Late December 1942 or early January 1943 we loaded on box cars which gave us a very uncomfortable ride up to the Tunisia front. We were packed into the box cars and had very little room to move around. In WWI the Doughboys called these box cars, forty and eight, forty soldiers and/or eight horses. There wasn't enough room for everyone to lie down at one time. Our first action was in the Qusseltia Valley (Kairouan) and for weeks we went back and forth up and down the front to cover hot spots. Committed into action on a piecemeal basis at company and battalion size operations and most of the time without adequate support. (As noted by Colonel Belisle in his comments, Appendix One)

My brother was in the Second Armored Division and some units of the Second were on the front in Tunisia. His Company, H67 and my Company made an attack in the Qusseltia Valley, but we did not have the opportunity or time to see each other. Later a mine injured my brother Jim, and he returned to the states. Our units had attacked across the valley and to the entrance to the pass where we parted company. My Company made a flanking attack by going around behind a mountain and into the pass at night. The attack was very successful, we took the pass. The path around the mountain was very difficult so we left our packs, taking only weapons, ammo, and water. A few days later some of us went exploring back along the route we had taken to attack the pass; and discovered that the trail was a mountain goat trail. We chickened out when we saw how narrow the trail was and with many high, steep drop offs.

After we would take an enemy position, if the situation permitted we would go exploring, or scrounging. One of our favorite pastime was collecting weapons and ammo and then seeing how long the weapons would fire before they got so hot, they quit firing. We learned a lot from these just-for-the-hell-of-it, "experiments." We also learned that in an unrestricted space some powder will burn, not explode.

The Army had very unusual passwords and counter signs; such as Betty Grable, - Legs, or Hi-HO Silver, - Away. One of the greatest was SNAFU, - Damn Right (SNAFU, situation normal all fouled up, to most GI's another F word is used). We had to send men to the rear every night for food, water, ammo, etc., and guide the replacements up. Usually they didn't start back until dark and most of the time it was after midnight or much later by the time the detail returned with supplies. It was an undesirable detail, having to spend half the night or more with a dreadful load, stumbling around in the dark. This one particular night they could be heard griping and making quite a lot of noise. So our sentry fired a couple of rounds over their heads, just for the hell of it I guess; because everyone knew who they were. Anyway, it got their attention really quick. After the sentry fired, they started yelling, SNAFU - Damn-Right, SNAFU - DAMN-RIGHT, over and over. You can bet that we received a bit of instruction (chewing out) about how to use the pass word and counter sign, and noise. The WAPS and Krauts certainly knew where we were, but no harm done.

The night we pulled out of the pass it was windy and cold. When we got where we were going we just sacked out on the ground. It started drizzling, then it starting snowing. We were wet, covered with snow, and we almost froze. Life can be so miserable, most times we asked for it. Before we got thawed out that morning they rushed the Company to another pass for us to hold for a week or so.

Finally, the Division regrouped, and went back into the fight at El Geuttar and fought as a divisional unit until the end of WW11. At El Geuttar we got into all sorts of situations. For example, was an extensive Stuka bombing attack while we were moving up to attack the hills east of El Geuttar. The bombing was not as effective as one would think as far as casualties were concerned, oh! But it scared the living daylights out of us. The Stukas made an awful scary noise when diving to drop their bombs, and frightening is an understatement. We were climbing and scuffing for a while getting into position to dig the Krauts and WAPS out of the hills. After we had taken our first objective we set our defense for the night and I assigned the alert/ stay awake crew for our squad. One of the men on the first shift was a very good friend of mine. He woke his relief on time and that was the last time anyone saw or heard of him. For some situations I don't like to mention names. This excellent soldier was the first man I lost during the war. When we were at Ft. Devens he and I made a couple trips to Northern New Hampshire.

We saw a few dog fights, fighters and bombers were shot down over and or near us. We saw a JU88 bomber shot down by our fighter planes; and it crashed into the side of the mountain near us with a load of bombs and gas. What an explosion! The only plane I saw shot down in WW11 by US ack-ack was a British Spitfire. We also were the spectators of the largest tank battle of Tunisian Campaign. We were fighting in the hills and when we looked out into the large valley there were hundreds of tanks of both Kraut and American. At El Geuttar it was the bloodiest and deadliest fight of the war up to this time for us. Digging the enemy out of these bare and rocky hills was a most dangerous and a deadly proposition; you became an expert very quickly, or you didn't make it.

Just another amusing incident was when we took a hill one afternoon and as we looked to our front we saw eight or ten Germans at about fifteen hundred yards scrambling and trying to put distance between us. Frazier, a machine gunner and my buddy from Knoxville, Tennessee, was firing his machine gun at them and he had time to fire a belt or more before they disappeared around a hill. Frazier stared in disbelief and in confusion picked his machine gun up by the trigger bar with the barrel pointing down to the ground and said, "Damn, I can't believe that I missed the SOB's." He also couldn't believe that he forgot to unload the machine gun, and the round in the chamber cooked off, blowing up a cloud of dust. Frazier though the Krauts had dropped a mortar round on him; he was so scared, that he was speechless. Believe it or not, about the same thing happened on Flat Top Hill in Sicily; at the same time the machine guns were firing at the retreating Germans I was trying to zero in the mortars. We could not see where the mortar shells were landing. I knew something was wrong, I looked up and saw that we were getting tree bursts. Very embarrassing. There was so much scrapple zinging around and so many shells coming in and going out that we didn't notice the tree burst at first. A few minutes later as we were thinking and discussing how lousy our fire was, a round cooked off in one of the machine gun, once again, scared is an understatement. This took a few more years off our life.

Slowly we took hill after hill as we advanced in the horseshoe shaped mountains east of El Guettar. We had just taken a hill in the early afternoon when we saw two German ME109s chase a Spitfire. The smoking Spitfire flying very low, came down the small valley or a wash, on our right flank. The pilot belly landed the plane and as it stopped skidding he popped out, hitting the ground running, away from his plane as fast as he could. He was thinking that the Germans would fire at his plane. The German planes made a pass or two over the downed Spitfire and left. Lieutenant Mock, (Staff Sergeant at this time) me and a few others, rushed down to get the pilot. He was very happy when he saw we were American GIs. The pilot thought he was in German territory; it had been only a few hours earlier. I don't remember the pilot's name, I do remember he was a First Lieutenant from Chicago, Illinois. We sent the Lieutenant to the rear as soon as conditions allowed. Then later that afternoon two ME109s returned and with a short burst of 20mm set the Spitfire on fire, it burned on into the night.

This article written for the Albany Herald, March 1993, to Commemorate FIFTY YEARS AGO, (MARCH - APRIL 1943),

Battle of El Geuttar

The Tunisian Campaign was a turning point for the US Army, particular the First Infantry Division, "The Fighting First," "The Big Red One." The invasion of North Africa was the start of combat for Army Ground Forces in the European Theater. Even though the invasion was a success there were many problems that came to light during the operation. The lack of logistical support, defective-inferior equipment, poor planning, and just plain stupidity went on into the Tunisian Campaign. With good fortune (or luck) our landings in North Africa were successful. Success was not the norm in the first few months of the Tunisian struggle. We were knocked around rather badly.

The Brass sent us into combat in a piecemeal fashion. We (The Big Red One) were used as a "fire brigade," committed at Company and/or Battalion strength along the entire Tunisian front. With much fumbling around, bad judgement, bad planning, unfamiliar senior commanders, and once again, just plain stupidity; most of us did survive and learned by costly lessons, the art of a Doughboy's combat and survival.

The Ninth Infantry Division took over positions held by The Big Red One about the 10th of March, and then the entire Division was finally assembled at the Tebessa-Marsott area. The task was great getting reorganized, new equipment, replacements, all desperately needed as we had suffered considerable casualties during the past few months. All this, plus pep talks, and constructive criticism (a little chewing), preparing us for the bloody struggle at El Geuttar.

The maneuvering for position began about the sixteenth or seventieth of March. On the twentieth of March the do or die attacks began. After seventeen days of constant fighting of the roughest sort, the First Division had proven itself to be an elite fighting force. The struggle for these horse shaped hills east of El Geuttar went on continuously, from jockeying for position and maneuvering to dig'em out to deadly struggles. Early one morning we made a successful move and captured the remnants of an Italian mortar position; they had been an important part of the enemy's hill defense. That day or the next the largest tank battle of the war at this time took place in the valley east of El Geuttar. The 1st Armored Division, plus attached units, fought the German armored force to a standstill, and won. Even though the 1st Armored Division was badly bruised they had proven they could slug it out with the best the enemy had to offer, and win. We were pestered something awful during this fight by the German air attacks, which petered out after this phase of the Tunisian Campaign.

There were many weird feelings while watching the life and death struggle of this tremendous tank battle. So many burning, smoking tanks, and life or death so close at hand in the hills, takes its toll. We silently cheered, bleeding internally, and grieving for our lost buddies, our comrades in arms. It was this time that we really learned to hate. This hatred for the Krauts carried through to the rest of the Tunisian Campaign, Sicily, France, Belgium, through Germany, into the Hertz Mountains, and Czechoslovakia.

After Tunisia we Doughboys had a superior attitude, never doubting our ability. We Doughboys of the Big Red One knew we were the best, second to none, I suppose we sorta proved it. The Big Red One, The Fighting First, wears the armor of history and the shield of tradition, heritage, the determination to succeed. The togetherness, "One for all, All for One," "No Mission too Difficult, No Sacrifice too Great, Duty First," the tradition of being the best; we asked and gave no apologies.

The Big Red One always moves forward, always takes its objective, never retreats. First in Africa, First in Sicily, First in Normandy and through France, First to enter Germany and breach the Siegfried Line, First to capture a German city, and on and on. There is no end to the exploits of the DOUGHBOY, and the Fighting First Infantry Division, U.S. Army. HISTORY SPEAKS.

(signed) A Doughboy

A Doughboys Narrative ●

CHAPTER SEVEN
Getting Good, and We Pay the Price

After taking El Geutar, The American Army was able to advance and meet the British 8th Army coming up from Libya. The Germans were forced to retreat, along the coast to Northern Tunisia. It took us a week to travel north and participate in the final struggle to defeat the Germans and gain full control of Tunisia and North Africa. We were fully seasoned combat veterans and had earned the reputation as a damn good division. This reputation followed us through the entire war. "As second to none," we were proud and it showed. Maybe we were sorta lucky or something, or maybe we were good combat infantrymen, because we did not lose as many men as some units did and accomplished more. No bragging, just facts, and history speaks. I don't like to think of the number lost, because one is too many. Though my squad, I lost four out of a seven-man squad during the campaign.

Tunisia was the place of my first patrol, a detail that no one liked and everyone dreaded. A reconnaissance or combat patrol, is sorta like being a scout, a very, very hazardous job. My first patrol was a three-man reconnaissance, with Miller, a French Army Captain and me. Miller was one of my best friends, buddy, and chum, really the best friend ever. Miller (from Johnson City, Tennessee) and I started out together at Ft. Benning. The captain, who was with our unit for a few weeks. He knew the area well and went with us on this patrol. Our mission was to find the German positions and detect their strength in a certain area. The three of us left a couple of hours before dark to get into position to scout along the foothills where we were to attack in a couple of days. We roamed along the base of the hills but we didn't find any Krauts. We were almost sure that they were around, but they made sure that we did not make contact. It was an all night ordeal, very nerve wrecking. We did not get the information that we needed and wanted. Twenty-four hours later we attacked the same hills that we had scouted out and we got clobbered with artillery and mortar fire. We lost several men caused mostly by artillery and mortar fire.

The final two weeks of the Tunisian Campaign was fierce, bloody, and with much agony. A combat infantryman is involved in many gut wrenching incidents. A few days before the end of the campaign we were caught out in the open in an artillery barrage. As the Germans started shelling us we scrambled up into some crevices and rock out-cropping trying to find some form of cover. Near where I was one of our men (I knew him well) was hit and I went to help him. The Germans were still shelling us, a shell came near and I fell to the ground a few yards from him. I rolled over to him and he looked at me and pleaded, " Help me, please shoot me." He died in a few seconds and I never knew in what way he wanted me to shoot him, with morphine or a gun. He was in extreme misery. We doughboys carried a syringe of morphine in our first aid kit to use if needed when we were hit in combat. In the next attack another buddy was hit and died as I as tried to help him. Tragedies such as these almost got to me many times. There are untold gut wrenching incidents that I do not desire to relate, nor remember.

Story time again: You have seen parades celebrating various victories but you hardly ever see the combat infantrymen, The Doughboy, in these parades. The fighters, the ones who took these cities in the first place; such as Oran, Algiers, Tunis, Palermo, and Paris. After the capture of Bizerte and Tunis we were still in the hills licking our wounds. During the parade in Paris the First Division was approaching and crossing the Seine River east of Paris, and slugging it out with the Germans. You just didn't see the takers, the doughboys parading. Company E 26th Infantry was never in a parade celebrating these events. I suppose we were not presentable, we were the ragged, dirty, stinking, undisciplined rascals. Uncivilized, according to Eleanor Roosevelt, who said that about The First Division, so there was no love lost between her and the First. General Teddy Roosevelt and Eleanor were related, family, but we still didn't like her for what she said about us, the Big Red One. During a visit with the troops of the First she made a remark, that it might be advisable to quarantine us for six months when we returned to the States, we booed her. When she returned to the States she, in a casual remark overheard by a reporter said, that "The First Division was uncivilized." Some considered that a complaint, even coming from her; for we of The Red One fought to survive; being civilized was not high on our list. It is difficult to insult a Doughboy, but it is easy to make him angry. Anyway we never paraded to celebrate our exploits.

This article was written for the Albany Herald April 1993. FIFTY YEARS AGO, TUNISIA, NORTH AFRICA, 4/23 Through 5/13/43

The defeat of the Axis in Tunisia was considered to be the turning point of the ground war in The European Theater. The performance of the US Army at El Guettar and later in the rugged mountains west of Mateur was also the turning point for the US Army. Up to that time they were a bewildered bunch that couldn't seem to do anything right. The men fighting in company and battalion size units, scattered along the entire Tunisian front felt forgotten. With no regimental, or division headquarters, it was disastrous. The results were, to get knocked around something awful for the first few months of the Tunisian campaign.

The enormous task of moving an Army to northern Tunisia over just one or two roads, rough mountainous ones at that, was a gigantic feat in itself. In the mountains west of Mateur, the last battle of the campaign commenced on the 23 April 1943. The British First Army had been unable to crack the German defense and here is where the unexpected happened that General Alexander, the combined Ground Forces Commander had not believed possible to accomplish. General Bradley's US Army 2nd Corps, consisting of the First, Ninth, Thirty-fourth, and First Armored divisions, plus some smaller units; with the RED ONE leading, they had broken the German defense and made it possible to capture Ferryville, and Bizerte; as well as the British capture of Tunis. The fate of the world renowned, cocky, German and Italian Afrika Korps was doomed and defeated 13th May 1943. Many of the American combat units were exhausted and well below full strength.

Up to that time it was the greatest defeat of the Axis since the start of WWII. The successful invasion of North Africa, the victory at El Geuttar, the defeat of the famous

Afrika Korps; capturing over 250,000, and gaining control of North Africa; how sweet it was, but still a long, long way to go.

signed, A DOUGHBOY

With fighting over in Tunisia we camped near an Air Force Base close to Constantine, Algeria, from which missions were flying over Sicily and Italy. Waiting for transportation back to Oran we didn't have much to do. We would visit the fly-boys and tell war stories. We were just plain curious as to how they operated. We were able to trade for or liberate a few goodies which we were hungry for, not having any of the extras for ourselves, that the Air Force seemed to have. (Appendix One, Colonel Belisle tells about our machine gunners going on bombing missions.)

(RHL. One great thing in this bivouac as we rested, was that we were taken by the truckload to the local hot springs for which Constantine was famous. We could soak up the hot water for about an hour and this was heaven for the doughboys who had been so long dirty and so long without a shower).

Staff Sergeant Mock and I became acquainted with a pilot and, Mock cooked up a deal for an airplane ride. The pilot and copilot wanted a carbine and all we had to do was to figure out how to get a couple. The men in the 4th platoon and a few others in Company Headquarters, including the CO and the first sergeant were the only ones in the Company armed with a carbine. We weren't about to part with ours and certainly weren't about to swipe any from our platoon buddies, so that left the CO and the first sergeant. It wasn't hard to decide. One day while everyone was at chow, we slipped into the CP tent and swiped two carbines; and took off for the Air Base to pay our fare for a plane ride.

The pilots were to fly that afternoon on a plane that just had a new engine installed. They agreed to take about six or seven of us. Mock and I got the bombardiers compartment up front, we had choice seats, kinda crowded, but a perfect view. Choice seats we should have had as we paid the fare. (By stealing or rather "transferring" two carbines). The others were in various places, as you may know there are no passenger seats on a B-25. This was my first plane ride ever. It was a great ride with a few dips and dives thrown in. Weightless was something that I didn't know anything about back in the forties. Certainly: it was worth two measly carbines. As an added bonus, we got a big kick watching them at company headquarters looking for their carbines, kinda hush hush like.

Later eight or so of us Fourth Platoon buddies hitched-hiked to Constantine just to be adventurous and to look around. Constantine has wonderful scenery, but doesn't have much in the way of entertainment for GI's; such as, booze and girls. Late in the evening we started thinking about returning to camp, but there wasn't much traffic going our way. This presented a problem, so we requisitioned (stole) a British weapons carrier. We got lost on our way back to camp and in turning around we got stuck in a ditch. As we were attempting to push the vehicle, the driver (don't remember who), stalled the engine. The truck rolled back into the ditch and pressed Meyers, (I think it was Meyers) against the bank, injuring his hips and pelvis. A satisfactory explanation to the Brass was difficult, we were convincing enough to keep from getting into trouble. I found a 38 Smith & Western pistol under the seat and kept it till August 1944, I kept the pistol plus other souvenirs in my small bedroll. All were lost when I was wounded.

We finally got transportation (boxcars, 40 & 8) back to Oran. The boxcar ride hadn't improved a bit. Most of the Fourth Platoon NCOs almost got busted, (reduced in rank) as result of rowdiness during the trip. We stopped along the way for water, coal, and a train crew change when lo and behold next to our boxcar were barrels and barrels of vino. Quickly grabbing a few water cans (five gallon size) and a pick mattock, (entrenching tool) we proceeded to help our selves. (More liberation techniques). It wasn't long before we were painless and brainless. The day after arriving at Oran the Commanding Officer lined us up and started chewing us out. In just a moment he stopped, eye balled us and said, "I've been with you men ever since I entered the Army, (Summer 1941), I was your platoon leader, I was your XO, and now I am your CO. I have never been so disappointed in anyone than I am in you guys; If I could replace you, I would bust every G.D. one you. Get out!" That is the only time I ever saw him angry or use fowl language. He was the best Officer I ever knew. I believe what made him so angry was that as we rode along on the train we would fire at "Arabs," just to see them jump! We were good shooters, we didn't hit anyone; or he could have gotten details of our plane ride or, the Constantine escapade, or the missing carbines, or the flatcar escapade in Algiers. On the trip from Tunisia to Oran about ten doughboys of the 4th Platoon with all of our gear moved to a flatcar that was on the rear of the train. We had plenty of room on the flatcar but when the train got to Algiers at night, they uncoupled the flatcar. We heard the train moving out, but we weren't moving. We had to make haste to catch the train, leaving some of our gear, two or three left their weapons. For a soldier that is an unforgivable mistake. We were in heap big trouble. Severe punishment was certainly justified. About the only thing we took seriously in those days, was saving our butts. Escapades of this sort were common, and combat Infantrymen were just down right ornery anyway.

The First Division troops were a little rowdy at Oran. Too much vino, too cocky, and too much steam to blow off. Maybe the British had the best description for the

Yanks or GIs, that's, they were over fed, over paid, over sexed, and over here, (England). We really picked on the noncombatant service people and had a lot of "fun" with the MBS people (Mediterranean Base Section). For the GIs there are many unprintable meanings for these letters. We wouldn't let MBS MP's take First Division soldiers in, and we were just plain disrespectful to non First Division people. We also received bad press on our being so cocky, and rowdy, resulting in some units being restricted. We had a very bitter fight for North Africa. We felt as if we owned it and did not want anyone harassing us about petty things. We just plain didn't give a damn for anyone or anything. The desirable entertainment areas where six months before we roamed freely, was off limits, enforced in a way that we couldn't get by the MPs.

We didn't stay in Oran but a few weeks, just long enough to get a bad reputation. We boarded the sister ship to the Leonard Wood, the ship that we were on for amphibious training in NC in 1941. We made a few practice landings on the coast between Oran and Algiers and finally made camp about ten to fifteen miles west of Algiers. We were in a scenic wooded area and the weather was tolerable to LOVELY. We had afternoons off and had a few fun trips into Algiers, where we mingled and met a few British 8th Army fellows that we shared a few bottles with. They were just about as crazy, daring, and cocky as we were. They also got into as much trouble as we did. We would go into the Casbah (of course the place was off limits, as were all places the GI would consider entertainment areas); we bought champagne at about seventy-five cents a bottle and really had a whooping good time. The Casbah had a few places called by some, a GI's delight. That was the reason that it was off limits; besides it was a dangerous place for the soft hearted. Most of us were loose as a goose and didn't have a care in the world, enjoy today for tomorrow who knows . . .

CHAPTER EIGHT
Sicily It Gets Tougher

I will insert a talk about the landing in Sicily that I wrote for a WWII Commemorative Program Services, 4 July 1993.

My talk today I hope will show our love and devotion for our family and our country. Maybe, we will see the contrast in our society, of the past and the present.

Our Commemorative Program is about the invasion of Sicily, 10 July 1943. The U.S. Forces were commanded by General Patton. The British Forces commanded by General Montgomery. To make the invasion real to us, I want to tell of it as an Infantryman would see it. I will try to paint a word picture for us. I want us to imagine or fantasize that we are infantrymen, Doughboys, and that we are in North Africa mid 1943. Let our imagination take us back, but I don't want any of us to get seasick.

The landing at Oran is history, the bloody fight For Tunisia and the control for North Africa is a success. We are battle hardened veterans of these campaigns and we are selected for another invasion. We have trained and practiced for years, but still more training so that we execute the many things a combat soldier most do automatically. We are just about ready to do anything or go anywhere just to get out of the redundant training and dry runs. We are told we are the best, and that we will get better; we believe it, the bad part is that we have to prove it.

The Battalion made a few practice landings on the coast of Algeria. Amphibious training is tough and exhausting, it makes you rubber kneed. We have to off load by going down a 20-30 foot cargo net with all our equipment into a small landing craft. Climbing or descending the net is most tedious, because the LCI is wallowing and bouncing around like cork, you more or less have to drop into the boat at the precise moment; if not there is a jarring collision between you and the boat. There is always danger of getting in between the ship and the LCI. Another pitfall is the cargo net, it is easy to get tangled in or your equipment hung up. As we complete amphibious training we go directly into more conditioning, weapons and tactics training.

About 5-6 July we stop training and began checking equipment, get extra ammo and rations, until we feel like a pack mule, and weigh just about as much. A lot to sink with, or lug around. The life of an infantryman is a life of extremes anyway, either not enough or too much. No food, no water, no support, no rest or free time. On the other side there is too much training, too much to carry, too much harassment, too hot, too cold, always hurrying or waiting, nothing never ever just right.

About 7 July we board the ship and head out into Mediterranean Sea and the briefings began, where, when, what to expect, etc. The beach east of Gela, Sicily is the place, we were guessing Southern France, Italy, Sicily, in that order. We check equipment again, making sure everything is ready. We have anxiety, dread, hope, wishing that we could be someplace else, because we know there is enemy defending the beach. The day before we are to land the weather turns against us, high winds, very rough seas, with 20-30 foot waves. Most everyone gets seasick, rumors are that the invasion would be canceled. In our favor is the enemy will not be expecting us to land in such terrible weather. Late evening the sea abated some and we continued toward Sicily. About midnight the cooks had only a few takers for chow, most were still too sick.

Next getting our equipment and going to our loading station we could feel the pitch and roll of the ship. Rough seas and darkness means we are in for a miserable few hours and nothing good to look forward to. After a bit of fumbling around we are loaded and we cast off. We form a circle and when our wave is complete we form a line, head for the beach at full speed. We get a lot of spray and get as wet as one can get, and sicker, and sicker. At about two thousand yards or so from the beach a search light tries to light us up. Thanks to our Navy friends, they very quickly blow it out. About five to eight hundred yards out we began to receive small arms fire. We have a few hits on our boat, our feet get itchy, but we have no place to go. To a Doughboy, movement is security, or it seems so. Also there is a small amount of big stuff coming in and going out. All of us are miserable, anxious, jam packed, over loaded and wet, most are sea sick with no place to be sick except on one another. There are no heros, just misery. Most don't much care what happens, just get it over with.

We feel the sudden bump as the boat hits an offshore sand bar, in a moment or two we get over it and hit the beach. The ramp drops, we hit the surf hurrying to get off the beach and into the sand dunes. To add a bit of drama there is a mad scramble as we are involved in a few fire fights. We make it across the beach and take a few yards of sand dunes. There are much excitement and anxiety, and a dab of fear because of the unknown. It is still dark, we take head count, get organized, check our location, we move out toward our objectives.

The first day or so is crucial for both sides and our main concern is to take our objective and dig in, and be prepared for the counter attacks that are sure to come. If we manage to hold for a day or so our chances for success increases. We over run our initial objectives and continue toward the airport and high ground, this will give us control of the beach. The Company has some success, but before we reach the objective we are counter attacked by tanks and infantry. We take defensive positions in a large ravine, that is a life saver for us. We take care of the infantry, but not the tanks. As more support arrives the situation improves. That night we start our attack for the high ground and airport. By the next morning we have taken our objective and many prisoners.

Of the many battles of the Sicilian Campaign I will tell you of one near the end. E Company lead the attack for a key hill near Torino. The maneuvering started the evening before, we got into position to make the attack and a little after dawn we had taken the hill, taking of this hill opened the way for our forces to take Tornio. The counter attacks started, with a total of thirteen in the battle for Torino. At nightfall we still held the hill, tho exhausted, mentally, and physically, with many casualties, we are troubled and hurt inside, we are bitter. We spent years training for operations such as these and it paid off, we are successful. We trained to the extent that in any situation we reacted instantly, without having to think. Our goal was to survive, this led to the destruction of things and people. Remember, we are very well trained combat Infantrymen, we have the will and means to destroy what is necessary to save ourselves and win, without remorse.

Actions I have described and the many thousands by our military do not come cheap. The costs were great, men that gave all, men that answered the call. What made these men want to perform so well? What is their motivation? General MacAurthur told us that it is, "Duty, Honor, Country." The Marines tell us, that it's "Always Faithful." The armed forces know how critical virtuosity is to the military. What is critical to the military force is also critical to a free society. Unfortunately, society is witnessing a collapse of standards.

Today we are celebrating the birthday of our Nation we remember people of the past and people today with prestige, dignity, and character, people that put "Duty, Honor. Country" first; people held in the highest esteem, such as, Kennedy, Eisenhower, Carter, Desert Storm Veterans, Bush, and others. And yes, this congregation. It has been said, we Christian Americans have been sleeping, as a result we have politicians, masters at misstatements, telling a bigger lie today; so we will forget the lie of yesterday. Politicians that support perverse people, such as the anti life, ultra liberals, militant homosexuals. They are appointed to high staff and cabinet positions, they tell us these people are, quote, "just normal and ordinary Americans." These same people are pushing for dangerous changes in our laws, and schools. They want to issue to our school children, condoms, instead of teaching common decency; they support alternative life style teaching, they are trying to make it a crime to protest against abortion. They say they are politically correct, do we believe this? All of this is being forced upon us, It is frightening! We do not, repeat, do not want to be used in these so-called social programs, or experiments.

We should pray that the President will seek God's guidance; and protect him from the sorry advice he is getting. We should wear our traditions, our heritage, our honor on our shoulders, and dare, anyone to try to take these from us, and speak up for what we believe, and act.

I have read this Book, The Word, The Bible, plus many world histories of man, I have never, ever, ever, read where it says perversion is ordinary and normal.

I have a vision for my children and grandchildren, that they will have a chance to soar as high as they desire. I am convinced that it is much easier to soar with eagles than with buzzards.

I would like for us to reminisce on the celebrations of the 4th July's of yesteryear. In the late forty's and the early fifty's Fourth of July meant family and friend getting together; playing silly games, eating watermelon, home made ice cream, and fried chicken. We all have celebrated the 4th in various ways. For me in the earlier forties it was a parade in Boston or Springfield, and be invited to picnics and a cook-out afterwards. I cannot think any country that has the freedom and opportunities that we Americans have.

We have no alternative but to return to the virtues of fortitude, diligence, economy, thrift, honesty, fidelity, duty and all the rest. This alone sees people through the hard moments in life. Without these, there is never, ever any freedom.

To conclude, with no apology when I say, we were good soldiers, just what YOU the American people made. Just as you made the Good Airman, just as you made the good Seaman, just as you made the good Marine, you the American People Made us all. Please don't you forget it. This is a point worth remembering. At this time will all veterans that served, that carried the torch please stand. Now all you young people look at these veterans and heros. Pick out your role model, for tomorrow you will be carrying the torch.

The old Army song says it for all of us, Old Soldiers Never Die, they just fade away. We will that someone takes our place. We have made what is here today. The future is ours. Will that we wake up! I salute you, and all Americans, for making us, the Military that we are. May God bless you and the U.S.A. THANKS

In addition I would like to elaborate on the first few days of the Sicilian Campaign. We had to do a lot of jockeying around to get in position to make the attack on the fortified hill near the airport. We started closing in for the attack about two or three in the morning. There was a tremendous amount of machine gun fire in our direction but we had very few casualties, it was as if the Italians were trying to miss, for as we closed they began to give up. McGrath, King, and I captured a dozen Italians. It was just getting daylight we were setting up our mortar when we heard a noise nearby, behind us in the ditch. Moving a little closer we saw twelve Italian soldiers, covering them with our weapons and indicating to then to drop their weapons and raise their hands over their heads. They were happy to be taken prisoner.

At times like these there is much apprehension, also many pucker factors. Sicily is all mountains; very, very rugged and I suppose what made it so bad was that we were continually on the attack. No stops, no breaks just attack after attack. It also seemed as if the Germans were more determined to hold Sicily, or delay the fall as long as possible. Anyway we had more casualties and many were my friends and buddies. After getting inland a bit it wasn't much of anything but just very rugged bare mountains, more or less bare hill after bare hill. Most of our attacks were started at night, so that we would close in and make contact at daybreak. It is very costly to make daylight attacks in open country. We put to good use some of what we learned the hard way in Tunisia. The last attack was the most costly in Sicily, losing about half of the Company. The last attack in Tunisia was also our most costly encounter of the Tunisian Campaign. The reality began to sink in, that combat is misery, misery, and more misery, with hell thrown in. This misery, this state of almost complete exhaustion takes its toll. Misery, fatigue, and fear cause some to become what we doughboys call "shell shocked." The doctors call it combat fatigue, combat exhaustion, and for General Patton it was coward and other words. Anyway it was bad, sometimes men lost all their senses, were mute, would cry, or just mumble. I have heard that it took some a long time to overcome this condition. Strange that I have not read or heard more about it.

General Patton was our Army Commander in Sicily as he was in Africa and really he was not very well thought of by some of us. We called him, "Blood and Guts." Our blood and his guts. For that matter we had nicknames for a lot them (officers), and in general we thought that the officers were pampered and not many were our heroes. Very few officers made lasting impressions on us (me). I had about half a dozen platoon leaders during the war and I remember only three. Two very outstanding officers, and one that almost caused the loss of the platoon twice in one day. And some, just officers. As far as the company commanders go I had the same amount, six COs, and only two, maybe three, the others as Company Commanders weren't worth a damn. So you know the reason (I think and so does the Army) that the NCO is the backbone of the Army. Of course we are and were a little prejudiced.

I have read many accounts of the various operations that we were part of, and there is very little that I can agree with. Even some of the official reports are not correct. Most all were written by officers who wanted to make them selves look good; or cover their own butt. Writers, reporters; most but not all, write in a Hollywood style, they give it a little glory and glamour with officer heroes and usually in a very flamboyant style to the extent of being absurd. There is no way to write about combat as I know it in WWII as being glorious, attractive, or desirable. It is very hard to explain the misery, tension, and hurt. In fact for me it is impossible to relate this misery, tension, hurt, and feeling for your buddies. Provided that you had a guarantee of life and limb it might be different.

I don't like the way that most reporters and writers describe the action of military people involved. Calling an officer by name, if one is anywhere near, and for enlisted men, neglecting to give their names. Using just men or enlisted men is not kosher. In most all action, repeat, all action, the riflemen and squad leaders lead the attacks, not the platoon leaders, nor was it the company commanders. They lead, but not in front. While the rifleman and squad leader were slugging it out with the enemy most of the platoon leaders and company commanders were in a much safer place. In histories of units there are pictures of all the officers and only a few pictures of enlisted men. As for me, praise, recognition, and awards cannot be over emphasized for these DOUGHBOYS, the RIFLEMAN. It may be just a pet peeve of mine, but to me it is valid. I served with hundreds of officers some earned my respect, many didn't. It has been my yardstick that the President and Generals have my respect automatically. Now, November 1992, with the lying draft dodger becoming jefe, this automatic respect certainly doesn't apply for me at all.

Let's get back to Sicily. We walked out of the hills to a small town in the northeast part of Sicily to wait on transportation. Not knowing when or where we were going and really we didn't give a damn. We knew it wouldn't be the States. I do know that we were quite solemn, hungry, tired; a ragged and dirty group of doughboys. The infantryman has a nickname "doughboy," that might describe us, we were a group of doughboys with no expression, just a moving faceless body, almost could be considered sorta shell shocked. Thirty-seven days of continuous walking, attack after attack, or being attacked. Remember that in one day we were attacked thirteen times! We were glad the campaign was over, but there was no celebration for us, we were still thinking of the misery, and our missing buddies. Of the two hundred ten or so in the Company when we left New York, 2 August 1942 (now August 1943) our original number had been whittled down considerably. I don't know the exact number for the company. Out of the nineteen that took basic with me only five remained. But the company had about 60% loss in Africa and Sicily. I suppose this was or could have been the reason we did not much give a damn for any thing or any outsider. The loss of our friends and buddies could not be justified or explained to our satisfaction, especially if it came from some noncombatant nerd. Soldiers grieve too. At this time you begin to think one might have been better off if they had been wounded way back down the road. A million dollar wound seem desirable at times.

I do not recall just how long we had to wait for transportation but we finally went to an almond grove about ten to fifteen miles west of Licata. Nearby was a vineyard, almonds and grapes go well together. We could not have planned for a better campsite. If it had to be in Sicily we could not have chosen a better rest area. We rested, trained a little, ate almonds, grapes and drank vino when we could get it. Wine wasn't too plentiful in this area. Time for the cheese story to go with the wine story back in Oran. We would trade for wine, snails, and round flat loaves of cheese from the local people. Late evenings we would sit around, eat cheese, snails, drink wine, and shoot the bull. We would throw a handful of snails on burning wheat straw, and suck them out of their shells. Eat good cheese, sip lousy wine. These were rather happy and blissful occasions. Quite a feast until someone sliced off a hunk of cheese, and when the loaf flipped over, on the bottom were lots and lots of maggots. We didn't know how to cope with this. Needless to say we were sort of pukey. Yuk! Some had to pick hair out of their teeth.

After the Sicilian Campaign was over, the struggle for Italy began at Salerno and for a while it was nip and tuck, (the Big Red One wasn't there). At times we thought we would eventually go to Italy, so it was on our mind quite a bit. Luckily the Allies finally got a toe hold so we rested some more, ate snails, cheese, (no more maggots tho, Doughboys sometimes learn quickly), almonds, grapes, and drank wine. In October we got word that we were leaving but we were not sure where we were going until we boarded the ship HMS Star of India (or it could have been the Bombay) that was going to Glasgow. Going to England was sort of a mixed bag, we were happy to be going to England but not too happy to be selected to lead the invasion starting the second front.

A Doughboys Narrative ●

CHAPTER NINE
Preparation For the Big One

After what we had been going through for the past year this was a fun trip and we had to make the most of it. Not enough room to do any training on the ship. It was almost as crowded as the Queen Mary. If the chow had been better it would have been great. A Doughboy must have something to gripe about. On all of the British ships that I was on the chow was awful. We had wonderful weather all the way, we played cards, shot the bull, got our ration of tea and crumpets in the afternoon, and relaxed. I couldn't believe we were drinking tea, for when we arrived in Scotland in 42, tea gagged us. Maybe we had lost some our taste buds. We socialized with the Brits, Singhalese, and some Indian soldiers, told war stories, and generally tried to enjoy the voyage. Our final destination was Swanage, England a resort town between Bournemouth and Southampton. Arriving in Swanage our billet was a small four or five story seaside hotel; enough room for all of E Co. Sounds great and it was a good home, We stayed there until the following May 1944.

We noticed bales of wheat straw outside as we were getting our room assignments. We were thinking that maybe snails might be on our menu. When we got to our rooms, we found out what the bales of hay was for. Our new home had wooden planks for beds and on each was an empty mattress cover. So we had wheat straw mattresses and were glad to have them, much better than the rocks of Africa and Sicily. The Fourth Platoon was on the top floor and by the time we left the following May our legs were in fine shape. We even had bathrooms with wash basins, and tubs, class you bet!

We really liked Swanage, the people were friendly and tried to make us feel at home. About six or so of us staked out a country pub, the White Swan about three miles out of town. We got acquainted with the owner and the local regulars, who became our dart and beer drinking buddies whom we liked very much. It was too far out of town to walk so we had to catch the bus and the last bus back to Swanage was at ten o'clock. The pub also closed at that time. Sometimes we missed the bus, and then we walked back. With that walking, the five flights of stairs and scheduled training, we were in fine shape, leg wise that is. The six or eight of us from the Fourth Platoon went to the White Swan Pub just about every night if money was available and if we were not training. The pub was closed on Sundays and we just played cards or a little football.

There were not many girls at the pub, so we played darts, drank beer, and swapped stories with the locals. On the bus I noticed a pleasingly cute young girl. All of us noticed her, she was what the GIs called cute, a knockout. At first she would not have anything to do with any GIs. Somebody must have talked to that girl. After a week or so she cautiously began to let me get acquainted with her. Gradually I learned; that she worked in Swanage and was evacuated from London during the Blitz of 1940, almost seventeen, (I was nineteen). She would get off the bus where we did and I would walk home with her every evening. I became attracted to her and she seemed to like me a little bit, I guess. Anyway we enjoyed each other's company. I did not correspond with her when I left Swanage for D-Day. When I returned to Swanage while in the hospital, November 1944, she had returned to London. I was unsuccessful in trying to get her address. I was sad and sorta heartbroken. Out of sight, out of mind, so they say. But that is not correct.

Our training in preparation for the invasion was very hard and consistent. The title of this chapter did not say rest, because in training as we did it there was none. Also we were very attentive and determined to get as much out of it as we could. Knowing that we would be in the first waves on D-Day we paid attention because we wanted to be the best of the best, which meant a better chance of survival. What we learned or did not learn could be the difference between life or death. In fact we were somewhat reckless not caring much for our bodies knowing that it was going to get rough with many uncertainties. We heard from people who made the raid at Dieppe, that was a failure, and saw pictures of it. We tried to learn as much as possible from them that had lived through Dieppe, a very bloody ordeal. So we knew what we were in for. We had learned back in Africa that expertise was survival. By Christmas we were settled into the routine of training and fun.

The Command surprised us by authorizing four day passes at Christmas for the Division. It would have been great except that we were just about broke as we had not been paid since arriving in Swanage. My good buddy and friend Sam Kessler from Cincinnati, Ohio received money from his folks and he insisted that I go with him to a resort east of Bournemouth. We were good buddies but still I did not want to spend his money and besides it would have taken a long time to pay it back. He said. "I will not let you pay it back, I want you to go with me and it will be, no payback." We went, and really lived it up big in a really plush resort full of old fuddy-duddy rich Brits, all very proper, us with two English ladies, hah! Hah, is for the word "ladies." We made an effort to charm them a bit, but I suppose that by fuddy-duddy rich Brit standards we were a bit crude, vulgar, and uncivilized. Later we had many laughs about that vacation. Kessler could put on a good act of being stupid or simple minded, this didn't empress them neither. We certainly enjoyed ourselves and spent quite a lot of money, about 500 bucks.

Lots and lots of training, forced marches (can to can't without stopping), much weapon practice and it seemed the weather was worst when we were out in it. One morning as we started on a two day (36 hours) forced march it began to rain. All that day and night, and through the next day it rained. When we returned late evening of the second day our feet were raw and sore, hurting so much that we could hardly walk, we were miserable. The training so intense that it slowed our pub going some. I guess we still had more time to drink beer than we needed. We had an exercise period first thing in the morning on a side street near the hotel (our barracks). There was a large two story house with large windows upstairs facing the street. Each morning there were two elderly ladies that would take exercise with us, they would do most of the exercises, but I would get them all messed up on the coordinating exercises. They were sorta entertaining, and it broke the monotony for us.

We enjoyed our stay in Swanage, our quarters on the beach (we didn't do any swimming, always too cold). Liked the area and the people were great. We had settled a bit, one couldn't believe that we were the same people that had raised so much hell in Oran and Algiers the summer before. While in England The First Division had a good reputation. The Brits would say things like; "They are not as rash as some Yanks." "Quiet, one would not know that they are combat veterans, they are not braggers." Their own troops said that we were, "bloody good." All of that going for us we were able to stomach the tough training and the homesickness. Sometimes we had Saturday afternoon and Sunday off and if we had the money, we would go to Bournemouth, which was a fine fun city. Just a few miles out of Bournemouth was the British Navy port, at Poole, that always had plenty of rum. They would sell it by the bottle to us GIs.

Late May, we moved to Camp Sir Walter Raleigh at Weymouth. This was a small British military base with a high ten foot fence around it. A few days before D-Day was scheduled, the gates were closed and guards were patrolling the fence. None of us combat infantrymen who were scheduled to go in on D-Day were allowed to leave the base. The only ones I knew that could leave the Base were the Chaplain and his driver. Briefings were given to us with the exceptions of location and time; which we received later. We were told of the expected defense. We knew and were told that it would not be a push over and to expect heavy casualties. Of course everyone took it in stride, trying not to think about it but we were very apprehensive. We were all sorta glad to forgo all of that hard, over and over training. It seemed as if the training had been as rough as it could be made so as to make us want to, maybe, do most anything just to get out of it, even combat.

These last few days we just rested and waited and waited, and waited some more with much griping. Would you believe we got paid? With nothing else to do but wait and grip, we gambled, mostly Black Jack. Sam Kessler, (one of my best friends and buddy) and I took the deal and got a hot streak and broke the game, winning about seven hundred dollars. That was a lot of money in 1944. There was no reason whatsoever to keep three or four hundred that each of us had, under certain conditions you can't take it with you, and their was no reason to send it home. Money didn't have much value at this late date to us. The Chaplain's driver slept in our barracks and he was the only person that we knew that could leave the compound. We got him to go to a place that we knew we could get scotch on the black market. At black market prices, about twenty-five to thirty bucks a bottle. We got two cases that took care of the surplus cash. The results was a big, big, noisy drunken party for the Fourth Platoon; we even had some to share with our friends in other platoons. It was a wonderful happy time, no squabbles, just fun drinking. I know that there are people (officers) that are still trying to figure out how we got so much booze, being that we were locked up tight. It always gave us much satisfaction to pull off something like this (like stealing the carbines). This all happened about the first of June and we were scheduled to start loading as early as the third of June, but we did not.

I think it was the fifth of June that we loaded onto the Landing Ship Infantry (an LSI carried an infantry company), all of E. Co. except the kitchen and supply was on this craft. Late evening 5 June, our LCI got underway and slowly threaded it's way out of the harbor. Weymouth Harbor was full of ships and craft of all types. It was unbelievable the number of ships in the harbor making ready to sail and as we got into the channel it was the same; ships as far as one could see in all directions. Quite a sight for a young country boy from L A (Lower Alabama). Getting dark there were patches of mist and fog, partly cloudy, but most of the time fairly good visibility. Of course we were very interested in weather conditions. Slowly heading south during the night, we saw hundreds and hundreds of ships and small craft. There was a huge amount of air traffic and a couple of times we saw transports and gliders.

The Fourth Platoon machine gun section was assigned to be antiaircraft machine gun crews as we crossed the channel. We had a good view of everything that was to be seen. As it became daylight we could see patches of fog and some clouds. On the beach (the coast of France at Normandy) were fog and smoke that would occasionally lift so that we could see some of what was happening. Ships, of all types, in all directions thousands of ships. A continuous roar of aircraft overhead, of all types. I did not see any observation aircraft though, but they were needed very badly, better observation would have been a lifesaver. We had lots of firepower but at times we were unable to use it because of lack of observation. It was the largest landing force assembled ever. If I had been a Kraut on the beach I would have probably filled my pants and fainted. Needless to say there was a tremendous amount of bombing, bombardment by the ships, and rockets; then the assault began. We doughboys were sorta solemn and we didn't have much to talk about, everyone to their own thoughts; this condition is normal in most nitty, gritty situations for a doughboy. A couple of hours after the initial assault began, we were close enough in our LCI to see some of the Kraut bunkers, and incoming shelling. Although visibility was not the best due to little patches of fog, haze and smoke, what we saw wasn't too inviting. We had a grandstand seat. As we watched we were bobbing around a couple of miles out waiting to land. We were hurting for our comrades, while dreading our turn that was soon to come. E Company was in the third wave and was scheduled to hit the beach at D plus 3 hours, about 0930 hours. On our beach Omaha Easy Red the situation was very, very unstable; and the result was that we did not land until D + 6 or 7 hours (about 1pm.)

Luck or events were against the First Division on this assault. The beach was one of the most fortified of all the landing areas. In addition the Krauts had just placed one of their first line combat divisions in the First Division beach area. They were conducting anti-invasion maneuvers and we did not know anything about the extra forces. Also about fifteen of the eighteen tanks that would be our support never got to the beach. Neither did the bombardment do as much damage as was expected, there were areas where there were no hits at all. And from what I heard and saw that there were nothing knocked out by the initial bombardment. The thoughts among us were that someone had let us down. The motto of the First Division that we Doughboys lived or died by was very evident. "No mission too difficult, no sacrifice too great, duty first." We had very heavy casualties yet we took our objectives and went further inland than anyone. On each side of the division, other units were four to six weeks getting anywhere close to on line with us, actually they never did. We were very proud of our achievements.

Getting back to our landing on Omaha Beach, it seemed that we would never get there. There was a lot of debris to dodge and on the first try we couldn't make it because of a partly sunken craft that the surf was moving near our LSI. We had to back off and try again. During all these happenings the LSI was attracting a bit of attention. LSIs have a ramp on each side that the troops use for disembarking. Just as we began to disembark the port ramp got knocked out. That really slowed us down getting off the LSI and our platoons got mingled, we did not want this to happen, at the very best it was chaotic. An LSI unloading troops is a big desirable target for the enemy.

The situation on the beach was anything but calm. The beach and exit from it still had plenty of mines of all sorts. Snipers, small arms, and artillery fire was still effective at times. After the problems of unloading our troops we were disorganized and we had very little space to regroup. One could not get out of the cleared areas due to mines. The number one priority was to get off the beach, get inland and take objectives. The area between high tide and the bluff was or seemed to be a solid mine field. I saw where mines had taken out ten of a twelve-man squad. It was not a pleasant sight; definitely a little demoralizing. We were very anxious to get off the beach. Men got hit while getting off the boat or while wading in the water. We still had to try to organize the best we could, quickly, in a very small area next to a draw that lead to high ground. Mines caused many casualties. Even with all the confusion and scattered pockets of the enemy; small arms and big stuff going and coming we finally started up the draw and into the woods and fields where we began clearing pockets of enemy resistance.

As we began to make headway inland and off the beach we began to feel better about our fate. To repeat, an assault on a hostile beach is like a one way ticket to a place you don't want to go. We were off the beach and had some room to maneuver; and, this is security to a doughboy. We moved inland that evening and on into the night and at about midnight we engaged a very strong road block of armored vehicles and infantry which we bypassed. Our orders were, reach our objectives as quickly as possible. This roadblock, the strongest point we had encountered was on a road with marshes and water on each side. And we had problems finding ways to bypass it. Our objective, was a road junction on the US Forces left flank. We hit many pockets of resistance during the night, but by the next morning we had our objective. This blocked the enemy forces from attacking the beach area from the east. We placed our all around defense at this point and waited for I don't know what, others to catch up I suppose or supplies, etc. Shortly after day break we heard a vehicle start up and it headed toward us on our left flank. It was still a little misty with a dab of drizzle and fog. At about one hundred yards we recognized the vehicle as a German half-track pulling an antitank gun. They came into our position before anyone could fire at them because of fear of hitting friendly troops. We were very surprised. At the road junction they turned right, back toward the beach, to our rear, where the remainder of our battalion was positioned. We were unable to fire, neither was the unit behind us. We would have been firing toward each other. As soon as the Krauts saw the troops they turned around after some problems, such as jackknifing the antitank gun. They had to unhook it from the halftrack, hooking it up again they came toward our position. They went straight down the road toward Bayeux through our positions and just about everyone got off a few rounds at the Krauts. But as far as I know they are still trucking, it was just unbelievable that we missed.

Later in the day we continued inland slowly. Road blocks and scattered pockets of the enemy had to be taken care of. We were doing quite well moving forward with light casualties. D+3 at midmorning we had cleared out a patch of woods when we got word that an armored/infantry column was headed our way. We stopped and dug in, or rather we went through the motions. Being exhausted the holes were rather shallow; we were not attacked, and luck was with us, because we were not prepared for an armored attack. We waited until about mid-afternoon then we received word that we could continue advancing toward our objective, Caumont. We were told that someone else had taken care of the Kraut armor. We continued to press inland as fast as the Krauts would let us; and of course we had a little to say as to how fast we went inland. The afternoon of the twelfth of June we were in position to attack Caumont, our main objective. I have always thought it was the tenth or eleventh of June, some sources say the twelfth. We had been on the move night and day since landing on Omaha Easy Red beach back on D-Day. Six days of contact with the enemy, continually on the go without sleep or rest except when waiting for something to happen. I actually saw men fall asleep walking. Men would stumble and fall or walk in the wrong direction; a picture of a zombie. We were moving and performing as the need arose, but we were more or less unaware of what was happening. I would suppose that fatigue or fear could have been the cause of our blank spaces.

We started our attack on Caumont about mid-afternoon and hit stiff resistance. My section did a fine job in supporting the assault platoons that afternoon, silencing a couple of machine guns that had the platoons pinned down. Later just before dark a couple of our tanks joined the fight that helped us advance on Caumont and get a toe hold. It was give and take during the night but by next morning we had Caumont, after cleaning out a few snipers and booby-traps. We received a few unsuccessful counter attacks and then did a lot of patrolling during our five to six weeks at Caumont. We were waiting for other units to catch up with us. (They never did). There was a truce in our area of the front, the Fourth of July to exchange prisoners. We Doughboys didn't think or much care about it one way or the other. This being the case with the infantry most of the time, our main concern was staying alive. All we were ever told was to go thisa way or thata way and attack.

Our 5-6 six-week defense of Caumont was rather quiet compared to the struggle on our flanks. The British struggle at Caon and the American struggle at St. Lo and Cherbourg. We had front row seats for the largest air assault on Caon in a ground support role. Later the air assault for the breakout of Normandy was the largest ever and we had front row seats again. It was quiet on our front most of the time after the counter attacks of the first week or so, except our front was shelled occasionally and got a few probing attacks. As we waited, we would do about anything to pass the time. During these quiet times occasionally all hell would break loose. One afternoon T. J. Cunliffe and I were sitting at the end of his foxhole playing cribbage. Suddenly we hear a SSS . . . Instantaneously I dove into his foxhole. Cunliffe was a little slow, so I was on the bottom and he was on top of me with his butt above the top of the foxhole. A piece of scrapple creased his butt. He was somewhat perturbed with me for taking over his foxhole, all in fun and in a good natured way. I told him I would scratch his crease a little more and then he could get a Purple Heart.

By no means were things uneventful in the wait for the flanks to catch up. My mortar section went out on a payback deal. The Krauts had previously set a trap for one of our patrols and got all but one. The one who returned, was able to pinpoint the German positions. So we planned and executed a pay-back that was successful. We placed our mortars out in front of our lines so they would be firing at their most effective range. We did this during predawn hours and then supplied the three mortars with 50 rounds of ammo each, using only a two-man crew for each mortar, normally the squad stays with the mortar. Mock, the platoon leader and Miller, the section chief (the three of us had been together since February 1940), were to direct and observe the firing from a point fairly close to the target. I was to control the firing of the mortars. At daylight Mock and Miller were able to locate the Kraut positions and Mock zeroed us in very quickly. Resulted in a wipe-out of the enemy positions with one hundred fifty rounds. We had to fire very quickly and get out of our firing positions before the enemy could react with counter fire, that did follow, but no damage. Our mortar section was very proud of our success when our

patrol confirmed how effective our fire was. While at Ca-
mount we learned that Mock was a very talented butcher.
Cows got killed occasionally and he would dress the cows
and there were good steaks for all. What a wonderful treat.
We didn't get steaks in England.

At Caumont, my good friend and buddy Miller ac-
quired a bottle of French brandy or something that was
very smooth, easy to drink, and from the results it was
very, very strong, about a hundred forty proof. We drank
the bottle rather fast and as we tried to stand we fell flat
on our faces. From that time on I became particular about
what I drank. Funny, amusing, and odd things happen in
combat that in spite of the situation you can laugh about.
One time I was trying to get as close as possible to the
enemy to direct mortar fire during the attack on Caumont.
There was some foul-up in distance between me and the
forward rifle platoon. They wanted mortar fire on a machine gun position and I was moving up to direct the fire
when a Kraut began firing at me as I was crossing a hedgerow. Needless to say, in an instant I was in a swan dive
off the hedgerow into thorny bushes and briars. A perfect
dive so I was told, me with many thorns and many
scratches. They seemed to think that we did a pretty good
job, I was given a Silver Star for my efforts. While at Caumont I located my uncle, Ray Spivey, from Red Level, AL.
He was a tanker in the 2nd Armored Division and I visited
with him a couple of times. It was a moral builder to see
and talk with someone from home.

A Doughboys Narrative ●

CHAPTER TEN
The Breakthrough, Wounded and Back At'um

Company E was relieved on the 14 of July and went back in reserve for about a week before we got into position to participate in the St. Lo Breakout, or Breakthrough. We received supplies, showers, and clean clothes; the first since landing 6th of June. I think a shower and clean clothes were really needed! We had gone much longer between showers so when it got to where we couldn't stand ourselves we would take a "whores" bath. Using our helmet serving as a wash basin, with a piece of undershirt or sox as a wash rag. Only a very small percentage of the body was washed, with special attention given to your feet.

A day or so before the breakout we moved again up to a few miles from the front. We were part of an armored Task Force, tanks were our primary transport and the plans were for the Task Force to move very fast, most of the time we did. Our experience attacking with tanks was limited, once each in Africa, Sicily, and at Caumont. We were beginning to think the tankers were not part of our war. A few times in the past as we were digging out Kraut strong points, which we thought the tanks should be doing, the tankers, after observing a bit, would say, "it might be antitank guns up there." Also we didn't care to be around the tanks because they attracted enemy fire. We were not overly enthusiastic about working with tanks. But starting with the Breakout of Normandy we worked marvelously well with the tankers. The tankers proved to be our life saver many times.

I cannot give much praise to the Air Force in a direct support role. I cannot recall one instance in our sector where they helped us Doughboys, with the Air Force being the deciding factor, in a direct (very close) support mission. One time we were cut off and the Air Force made an air drop of food and ammo and missed, and the krauts got it. The Artillery was our life saver throughout the war. I could never over praise them. As usual at times we did not receive the support that we thought we needed. But in most cases the lack of support was because of poor or no communications.

When H hour came all hell broke loose. Artillery shelling, bombers wave after wave, and fighter bombers strafing and bombing, over three thousand planes made the raid, the largest raid ever, it was unbelievable. Smoke started drifting back toward us and we received all sorts of odors. Then some jerk hollered "Gas!" What a terrible thing to happen, being that some had thrown away their gas masks shortly after landing on D-Day; for some their gas masks were up on a tank and not near at hand. You cannot imagine the panic. We finally decided that there wasn't any gas, only just a few years off of our lives. After what seemed like a long time (only three hours) we began moving out on tanks. The air attack was not as effective as we would have liked; once again, just like on the beach at Normandy, there were many areas with no damage. The push or race was to go all the way into Germany. The Company got to Germany in September. We didn't stop except when stopped by the Krauts. The Germans would set up road blocks and try to stop us or at least slow us down a bit. At times the action would be vicious and deadly. In all this our columns, American and German, would get mixed, we would meet a column of a few enemy trucks occasionally. We had to stop and shoot at each other a bit and then move on again. We did not have a lot of casualties in any one action and I contribute that to luck, or quick to react, or good at what we were doing, or probably all. In my reading history of other units I have noticed that some units were slow to take advantage or react to the situation.

We were in a lot of action, fighting every day and inflecting considerable losses on the Germans plus taking sizable number of prisoners. We did not lose a large number of men at any one action but with steady daily casualties it began to amount to a lot of people. One time we had just a short while before, fought it out with a road block and when finished we were in a column marching down the road when a Frenchman ran up to us jabbering and pointing toward a farm house and barn. We finally decided that he was trying to tell us that there was a Kraut soldier in the barn asleep. Miller and I went to check it out and sure enough there was German soldier in the barn asleep. We Took his weapon, woke him up, and took him prisoner. He was quite surprised and showed much fear. Our concern and fear were that there could be more than one. Most of the time we were riding tanks and when we met resistance we would hit the ground and attack. As a task force and spearhead we were quick to react, push them aside and keep going. The quickness of our attack probably was the reason that our casualties were considerably light compared to the action, plus we had great success getting our objectives. Later in Belgium and Germany our luck changed and the Company had tremendous losses and at Hurtgen Forest, where the Company was wiped out.

The 31st of July and 1st of August the Air Force had discovered a large German (division size, plus) column that was trying to escape from being trapped and captured. They were practically destroyed and late evening on the 1st of August we were right in the middle of all this mass confusion. It was the most chaotic situation imaginable. We were meeting resistance as we tried to advance, I suppose we would have met resistance if we had tried to redraw. At dusk we stopped and set up an all-round defense. There wasn't any such thing as a front. We couldn't tell how many or where the enemy was, because Krauts were everywhere. We were sorta in a tacky and precarious situation. We were in hedgerow country and in our perimeter was a wheat field that we did not go into. We stayed around the hedgerows so we would not be seen by the enemy observers. The Platoon dispersed along the hedgerows and connected with other platoons of the Company in an all around defense. Unbeknownst to us there were Germans hiding in the wheat field. About 1am they tried to make their escape, we at the Platoon CP were attacked first, killing two. Mock, the Platoon leader died on the way to the hospital. Miller, the mortar section leader died instantly. Magi, the platoon runner was slightly wounded, and I was also wounded. Other members of the platoon very quickly dropped the Krauts that shot us. The men of the platoon did not know that anyone was near until the Krauts started shooting. There was a lot of confusion for a while, to say the least.

I was stunned, or in shock for a few minutes after being shot at close range in the leg (the fibula shattered), across the left side of my chest and into my upper arm and out. I remember being hit, or vaguely the sting of the pain, but not where, or how many times; I was trying to kick the Kraut and reach for my carbine at the same time. After being hit the first thing that I remembered was the medic feeling around on my back in the darkness trying to find where or if the bullet that entered my chest came out. I heard him say that he could not find where the bullet came out. Needless to say that was of great concern to me. The medic bandaged me up the best he could in the dark and when I told him I was hurting and he gave me a shot of morphine. Stretcher bearers took me back to the aid station, on the way back they stumbled a few times in the darkness, but with a 1/4 gram of morphine I felt no pain. A doctor was examining Lt. Mock (my platoon leader) when I got to the aid station. Mock was very seriously wounded. Someone quickly checked me, then they sent us back to the field hospital.

Arriving at the hospital a little after sunup, as they were getting us out of the ambulance I asked how Mock was and a medic told me he was dead. In the past few hours two of my best friends had given their lives. As I reminisce a bit, Mock, Miller and I had been in the same platoon since 1940. What a waste! We had fun, trained, worked, planned and fought the enemy together for almost five years. In a way, Mock, Miller and a few others were more than family to me. They had saved my life a few times and I theirs. There is just no way to explain what and how we felt for each other. I tried to forget that I was hurting, even though I was in much pain and I was not out of the woods myself. I feel very low, now, as I write about this and while I am feeling this way I will add a little more sadness. During the many dangerous times and the good times as we took care of each other, our concern, our love, and our respect showed. By this time all had been whittled away from E Company. Mock, Miller, and I, were the last of the nineteen that joined E Company in February 1940. Without intent to brag, and with no apology when I say; during the many campaigns, we were a bunch of good soldiers, My buddies and friends that had dwindled away in Africa, Sicily, and France. I was the only one left and still in the Company in March 45, of this group of nineteen; all were wounded, killed, or were gone for various causes. We would often talk about how happy we would be, and what we would do when the war was over. It was over for many of my old friends, what would be my fate? By this time after our long road of combat, at times, it looked or seemed as if we felt nothing, we had no emotions, no tears, but we hurt; and it is hard, almost impossible for me to express my feelings. Today, July 1993, I get tears, I cry, and choke up with emotion, as I write this or think of some of the tragic happenings in which we were involved. No one can know the bitter hurt at times that has been with me for these many years. For years I made an effort not to think about it. Only one out of the nineteen that I have been able to contact. As I look back I remember how accelerated combat was; you started an attack early morning and then the next thing you remember it was late afternoon. I have many blank periods while I was in combat. Just everything seems out of proportion to reality. Back then and still today I have lost hours, days, places and towns during combat. I often wonder what caused these so-called blanks in remembering what happened, was it anxiety, exhaustion, fear?

On 2nd August 1944 I knew all the men in E Company, and most of the Company that landed on D Day. When I returned to E Co., January 1945, I knew only two. Only two, they had been wounded at least once or twice; two left after continuous combat for seven months had taken its toll. Approximately one thousand men killed or wounded in E Company. Combat is intense and contact with the enemy is short compared to the time that you are on the line. For instance Oran was hours, Tunisia and

Sicily were days and weeks but in France and Germany it was months of continuous contact, with many casualties.

Briefly, when involved in an attack, or being attacked it is a period of extreme tension, anxiety, consternation, or whatever. At other times one is still in extreme danger of being shot at, step on a mine, air attacks, artillery and mortars, and again whatever. A doughboy is just about always under some form of tension and stress. Thus, the faceless, blank look and, the lack of feelings, is very common for the doughboys. I don't know of a DOUGHBOY that was on the line, that went all the way starting at Oran. Hurtgen Forest was the Waterloo for E. Company (Nov. 1944) when the Company was wiped out. Of course the soldiers of the field train survived (cooks, supply, sick etc.) and those in the hospitals. This was followed by the Battle of the Bulge where there was another 50 to 75 per cent casualties. Company E had been replaced many times over. January 1945 E Company had a mailing list of approximately one thousand. Usually personnel stayed on the list for six months.

Back to the time at hand, the field hospital was busy and over "booked." It was the next day before my turn came and by then a dab of infection had set in. After the doctors cut, scraped, drained, and a brand new cast; I was returned to my canvas cot. The next day they flew me to England, (my third trip to England), to The 192nd General Hospital close to Oxford. I had a rough time trying to adjust after being independent for so long, it was hard to have to depend on others. At times I had much pain and was given drugs. Because of this, plus the mental and physical exhaustion, I wet the bed several times. My bunk mate, a tanker, who had lost, (or had given) an arm and leg, and had face/head wounds also had the same problem. Our nick names were Pee in bed Number One, and I was Number Two. Just about every night the nurse changed our bed linen at least once, some times more.

What a life! And embarrassing too. Always with misery and a hurt here or there, because casts were too tight and it was difficult trying to get around with one good leg and one arm, hurting myself at times in these efforts of independence. Also, winding down from the mental hell of combat was a problem. I was not overly cooperative, harsh, and abrupt. After a few weeks it was time to try a walking cast. All was fine until I fell on it. The cast was crushed making it necessary for another one. The doctor tried to chew me out, because he had to work on Sunday, which sure worried me, like laughing in his face. Like I have said if you weren't of The Big Red One, you are nothing. Later still, about seven weeks, it was time for another cast. This time they broke the bone to lengthen my leg.

Early December I was dismissed from the hospital and went into a convalescent unit. It was during that time I visited Swanage again staying at the pub where we always went when we were stationed there. I became reacquainted with my friends in Swanage during my short visit but it was not the same without my Army buddies. To me the loss of my many close friends, buddies, and that sweet young lady is something that will always be with me. To this day I hurt when I think of the abundant good life snatched away from my buddies. That is war! It is very hard for me to think it can be justified. What a waste! Oh! What a waste! Why can't people understand that fact?

The Battle of the Bulge started 16 Dec 1944 and the desperate need for men increased considerably. Overnight the doctors decided that I was ready for combat again, stiff ankle and all. The doctors had indicated, and I thought too, that I would not return to combat. After getting equipment and clothing at a replacement center at Birmingham the return trip began and so did the misery. Across the Channel on a LST to Le Harve up through France and Luxembourg and to E Company in Belgium.

As I traveled through France snow was a few feet deep; and it was bitterly cold. I waited a few days for transportation in Northern France and I was already dreading being out in the boondocks again. We did not have the thermal underwear, the shoe pack boots, Gor-tex clothing, no space age stuff. We were miserable at all times and almost froze to death. Some did when they got wounded in bitterly cold weather. By January the Battle of the Bulge was about over, just a few more towns and lost ground left to be taken.

I caught up with E Company in January on a cloudy miserably cold evening just as they were getting ready to move out to make a night attack. I did not have long to sweat about getting back into the agony and hell of combat as a platoon sergeant of a weapons platoon. To me it was a mixed bag, I was anxious to see some of my buddies again, but the misery of an infantryman was something I would have rather do without. As I began to look for familiar faces and ask about certain people, I was bitterly disappointed; at this point I did not know of the many, many casualties or the loss of E Co in the Hurtgan Forest. You can never imagine the empty feeling, the hurt, the anger, the bitterness; finding out that they were all gone, wounded, KIA back down the road at the Bulge, Hurtgen Forest, Aachen, Belgium and Northern France. I did not know any of these men now in the platoon. It seemed as if I had gotten into the wrong unit.

It was very difficult, almost next to impossible for me to return to the art of survival. I was bitterly angry wanting revenge, while hurting with lonely feelings. Made it hard to cope with combat. I had a platoon of about 30 men (no officer platoon leader at this time, the number varied every day). Men I did not know and who did not know me. I knew my situation, I had to get the confidence and respect very quickly. Respect doesn't come automatically. One does not last long in combat unless you have the trust and confidence of the men you are supposed to lead, as well as team cohesion. If you say jump, they must jump; that's the confidence and respect you must have to survive. I, being just twenty, young for a platoon sergeant, could have made them uneasy. But repeating, I believed I was good at my job and I had the experience, knack or luck to do the right thing most of the time, this meant a better survival rate for all of us. I have always had this thought as I stood before a group of men; that standing in front of me, were men that maybe just as good or maybe better than I. That night after wallowing around in the freezing slush and snow we performed well, and took the town.

After the first attack we had a mutual respect and it grew, we were a team of good and determined fighters. It was my good fortune and theirs also when they saw I had the knack for doing the right thing at the right time. A lot of them had less than a year in the Army and were young, but now all combat veterans with a will to survive. The weather was bad for anyone outside. Snow, wet snow, sleet, slush and mud didn't make it ideal for wallowing around in. However, some of our best and fiercest fighting was during this period.

We would be attacking a town and would see the buildings that would seem to be most comfortable for us. Also we looked around we saw snow, slush, and mud everywhere. Our desire to get out of the slush and mud made us very, very determined deliberate fighters. We were going to take the town for reasons of comfort. We were making headway into Germany and at the Roer River we paused awhile to wait for the water to recede a bit and at the same time we were hoping for better weather as it was miserable. We waited, we griped, we knew that the Army doesn't need an excuse to wait, it comes naturally, they just do it. We were not on the line now so we made trips up to the river to look over the section where we were to cross. We had to be sneaky about it; the Germans were looking also. River crossings are sorta like beach assaults, very hazardous. It is an infantryman's dread and we expected to pay a high price at the Roer. Then, the time came. We crossed at night and to our pleasant surprise the resistance was light; we had struck the defense where it was only a scattering of pockets. We took our objectives very quickly and suffered only minor casualties. After crossing the Roer we were continuously on the move taking town after town and we got into a few brief very bitter fights. There was moderate too light resistance most of the time. Flat country with a canal or two to cross and a little snow at times, but mostly mud, cold, and slush.

As the weather began to improve some, with bearable days rather cold nights and still we preferred and needed towns for nighttime use. When we crossed the Erf Canal (I think that was the name, close to Liblar), we made a night/dawn attack on a town that was near the canal and it was freezing cold. As we crossed the canal at daybreak we got wet and were bitterly chilled. We desperately needed a place to dry out and get warm. Just as the advance platoon made contact with the German defense at daybreak, the reserve platoon and the Fourth had completed crossing the canal when every man start screaming and hollering, firing and running toward the town defenders. This completely demoralized them, I suppose that the Krauts were in shock as we ran through and over them. It seemed that we had the town and the few Krauts who were left did not know what was going on. For us it was a matter of fight or freeze. They were holding the town and we, the attackers had to cross an open field to attack. They had the advantage but we very quickly took control of the battle field. It took longer than usual to clear/mop-up the town. With several men I checked out a large bunker crowded with civilians, and we thought that German Soldiers were in it also. We ordered the soldiers to come out. The first one out made the mistake of reaching for, maybe identification, and one of our officers shot him. It was very smoky and I did not recognize the officer at that moment. I did not think it was necessary to shoot. I went over to where he was and punched him in his side with my carbine and told him if you shot him again, "I will shoot you." When I saw who it was I thought I was in big trouble. I was a doughboy with many personalities, but I was not just downright brutal. Very shortly we had much more to worry about, such as a very vicious counterattack of the sort that would make one forget most anything. We lost many in this attack. For my action in trying to beat back the attack I received the Bronze Star, that might have helped the officer to forget.

The weather made a sudden turn for the better which we greatly appreciated. Next was Bruhl, and we paused for about a day and a half there. We took Bruhl with a night/daybreak attack, it was lightly defended. It was a good one. We had preferred and perfected night/daybreak attacks. Bruhl was a good city for us, we were the takers and we took. After getting our defense set up on the outskirts of the city we started scrounging, or plain looting. We Doughboys scrounge or appropriate, noncombatants loot. We found lots of eggs, ham, sausage, bread, and of course kraut. To my delight, I found some pickled eggs and pickled pigs feet, yum yum. Our biggest find was a German Army Warehouse full of booze, wine, and canned goods. It was about ten or so in the morning when we found this warehouse. There were about four or five of us and we took as much as we could carry as samples back to the 4th Platoon. We received a good reception and the news traveled fast. We were questioned as to what and where it was and then quite a few men took off for the warehouse to get in on the plentiful supply of booze. Would you believe that by the time some of the fellows got to the warehouse they had MPs on the place? That was three or four in the afternoon. The speed that guards were placed on the warehouse reminds me of the famous few words seen just everywhere during WW11. KILROY WAS HERE! These words seemed to be on walls and buildings in the towns as we captured then. I have never figured that one out. Sorta perplexing.

Placing guards on the warehouse called for a strategy meeting. It was decided that we would send a couple of men around front to entertain the guards, while at the same time we would take the jeep (it had just arrived with ammo and supplies) down the railroad tracks to the rear of the warehouse and take what we wanted. This operation was very successful and goodies were enjoyed by the Company. On top of this good feeling about Bruhl, the good weather and there was a feeling that it would not be long before the end would come. Yet it was still a very dangerous lifestyle, as I have said before, we felt as if we were fugitives from the law of averages. There were still some vicious brief encounters which lacked the prolonged duration of encounters with the Krauts in the past. I am getting out of sequence with events.

After having experienced really fine weather for the past week or so, it was pretty cold the night we took Bonn; it was fairly easy for us to take. Surprising to us was the taking of the Remagen Bridge. The Brass rushed us as fast as possible to that area and we crossed the Rhine on assault boats (LCI) about a mile down stream from the bridge. After a couple of hours waiting, for I don't know what, we were given objectives of a few towns, an airfield, and a road junction. We did a fine job, in a reasonable length of time, in taking our objectives and met only moderate to brief, strong resistance. At the airfield and road junction we did receive heavy artillery bombardments. A couple of instances happened that are worth mentioning. A First Lieutenant was assigned to the 4th Platoon as platoon leader just as we were leaving Bonn. We had not had a platoon leader in months. He got the platoon cutoff twice in one day by leading us the wrong way. We had made a night/daybreak and a late evening attack on the same day. The survivors were very upset, in other words fighting and shooting mad; and it was my job to suggest to the CO to move the Lt. out or else. That was unpleasant for me to do. But in a few minutes the Lt. was out.

The last action that I was in during WWII, was the taking and holding of a road junction. We lost a mortar in this action. It was hit by artillery fire. We received some heavy shelling but we took the road junction at night. The Germans could not take the junction back but made sure that we were not able to advance. That was what all the shelling was about. That night there was a tremendous amount of tank movement on our front. The Germans were trying to prevent getting cut off. A German Army or so did not make the escape, over three hundred thousand were captured.

During the previous few weeks things were happening at a very fast pace. So much happening in a very short period of time till I would seem to lose track of days and even there would be blank periods of time that I didn't remember anything at all. I have often wondered if others had that happen to them. I know at times we would be talking about a particular incident, some would not know what happened. So I suppose we all had that problem, or good fortune depending on the way it was.

See APPENDIX FOUR, Manning'S NOTEBOOK AND "E" ROSTERS of December 41, Feb./Mar. 1945.

CHAPTER ELEVEN
The Long Awaited Day, Going Home

When the flanks caught up with us at this road junction, the Brass let us get squeezed out for a couple of days. We regrouped, got mail, ammo, clothes, and replacements; and to everyone's surprise we got paid! This was the first full pay that I had received since 1 Jun. 44 at Weymouth and now it was the last week of March. We did not know that we were getting ready for the final push of the war. When the E Company went back to the front in a couple of days they did not stop until they reached the Hartz Mountains and Czechoslovakia. About mid-afternoon 1st Sergeant Manning sent word for me to come to the Company CP, and that I was going to the States on R & R. I did not believe him as we kidded or harassed each other quite frequently. I thought he was kidding me. We had a sound power phone to the CP and my thinking was if it was true, he would have called me. Anyway after awhile the person on our end of the line hollered, "Sgt. Spivey, the First Sergeant wants to talk to you." It was Manning wanting to know why in the hell I wasn't at the CP. He said, "Get your butt down here if you want to go home!" That convinced me, and in no time at all I was at the CP ready to leave. There was no time for any lengthy goodbyes.

I did not have to pack anything, all I had was in my pockets. In my small bedroll were a few goodies and that was back with the field train. It wasn't worth much. The second quick departure. When I got wounded, I lost all my goodies, now the same. It is hard, almost impossible for me to explain my feelings. I wanted desperately to leave combat but hated very much to leave the friends and buddies that had been a part of me for the past few months. In leaving though it meant leaving the misery and numb feeling of the fear of death. Also the worst of all was thinking of many who did not make it. It is so easy to say, "Face reality." Such as, don't dwell on the happenings of the past, just suck it up, shake it off, and try to forget. Oh, easy to say but hard as hell to practice. Go home, forget yesterday, live today for tomorrow.

Sergeant First Class Francisco Antocicco (with three Purple Hearts) and I who had served together since Fort Devens. We were still a bit numb in disbelief as we moved off the front riding in a jeep back to Danger Forward (First Division Headquarters Forward). To our pleasant surprise we met Sergeant First Class Albert H. Currier who was a member of E Company at Fort Devens. Currier, Cunliffe, and Oakie Clark were transferred to B Company at Aachen. I was told that they got drunk and set some buildings on fire in Aachen, because they were angry with the Krauts. Who wasn't? About the same time B Company was just about wiped out and was desperately in need of men, especially NCOs. So instead reducing them, they were transferred to B Company. Clark, when getting close to the Krauts, in an attack, would yell, (a rebel yell if you please). This habit of yelling probably saved us from casualties while making an attack. The story is, the First and Second Battalions were attacking. The First Battalion was making a flanking movement as the Battalions met head on by mistake some one of E Company heard Oakie Clark yelling. They were able to stop the fight before too much damage.

Currier, Antocicco, and I stuck together throughout the trip. We were kinda quiet, not showing any emotion, and not celebrating. Now here we were just three infantry Sergeants who were haggard, hollow eyed, exhausted, mentally and physically, repeat, fugitives from the law of averages. I repeat there was no way that I could express my feelings, there were too many "buts and ifs." It was unbelievable and I had hoped for this moment so many times. The war was over for me, for a while anyway. It's times like this, when things are very important to me, or emotional, that I get to repeating myself. Over the past couple of years we (my dear friends and buddies) had talked many times about what we would do when the war was over and we went home. Our hopes, our plans, our future, things done for each other; and now the empty, lonely feelings that kept me from the joy that I had thought I would have. These thoughts lingered with me for a long time. It really did take a long time to put the war years into the background a bit. I was, or tried to be optimistic but the ghosts of the past were very real to me at times. I will repeat, do what you can, suck it up, go on living, try not to dwell on the past. Again, that is easily said, but...

We had an overnight stay at Danger Forward and then on to Danger Rear in Northern France, or it could have been Luxembourg. At Danger Rear we turned in our weapons, we felt naked without them. We began to believe that maybe we were going home, yet we did not celebrate. There they told us how to act when we got home. It was sorta amusing to be told to quit our vulgar, crude, blunt ways, particularly to zip our filthy mouth, and many, many other bad habits. For so long our thoughts had not been on how to make friends, we didn't much care what we said, or did, or to whom. You and your buddies were number one and to hell with everyone else. We did do a little "influencing," just ask the Krauts! The worst part about the talk was that it was true; we were crude and vulgar and as Eleanor said, "uncivilized." The fact was, we were combat soldiers with no promises of tomorrow and we didn't much care about anything or anyone, except foxhole buddies. We didn't care what anyone thought about us and were not very talkative. We kept most of our thoughts inside.

We left Danger Rear and went to Le Harve for about a week. We went into town once and drank some rot gut which was not worth going back for seconds We gave up on the idea of maybe celebrating a bit. We began to loosen up a bit, more talking and joking. We also shared what we planned to do when we got home. After about a week we boarded a transport and went by way of Southampton to take on some wounded, bound for New York and other points in the USA. We arrived midmorning after an uneventful crossing of the Atlantic. I was a very impatient fellow. It was slow getting off the ship, slow getting to Fort Dix and slow processing for 45 days of leave. Really everything went rather smooth and fast; haircuts, pay, uniforms with all ribbons, but it seemed like it was all too slow. Italian prisoners of war were working in the Fort Dix kitchens, warehouses, and doing cleanup. I and others I am sure, had mixed feelings; very bitter and resentful, thinking about the misery and the casualties caused by them back in Africa and Sicily. While we were in mud, slush, wet and miserably cold, slugging it out with the Krauts. The Italian prisoners of war were living a life of luxury here in the States. Yes, we were bitter toward them with no love lost.

Jim (my brother) was stationed out on Long Island, or so I thought. Getting my leave I went to Patchogue and there was no Jim, he had moved. I didn't know where he had gone so I woke the local postman and got his address at his new station near New Rochelle, NY, at Fort Solcom. Getting back into New York City I was tired of lugging my bag so I checked it at Grand Central Station and continued to New Rochelle. I woke Jim and Rose at about 4am and we talked until breakfast when Jim had to go to work. After a short nap I shaved, took a bath and I went back to New York City with the excuse to get my bag. But for real, I had promised myself that I would have a fling as soon as I returned to the States.

I got a room at the Hotel Taft, got my bag and left it at the hotel. Then I started getting serious about the fling by having a drink or two of loud mouth at a bar at Times Square. Then I went to a bar-restaurant, I think the name of the place was the Log Cabin. It was a short distance from Times Square and they treated me like a VIP, wanting to know my pleasure. They also questioned me a lot about the First Division. After a dab more of loud mouth I told the waitress and bartender that I promised myself a fling. This included a treat to a sirloin steak dinner with all the trimmings. I was in uniform with my ribbons and the Red One (the First Infantry Division) on my sleeve. They told me that my money was no good; said everything would be on the house, and they might scrape up a sirloin. And they did. Some units of the First were stationed in New York City and the record of the First Division was well known, and we had very good press in all of the Northeast. I was an honored nonpaying guest at the restaurant and customers kept drinks on my table. I could not eat or drink all that was offered to me. Somewhat ill at ease and embarrassed at the attention given to me; but I was also pleasantly pleased above all expectations at all the attention and wonderful treatment by these strangers so gracefully given to me. I even had female company, a couple of girls from New Jersey sat at my table and they were the hit of the night.

I began to feel that maybe I might be a hero of a sort. I will never forget these wonderful people and that terrific night. Later about midnight, remembering became foggy for me, the next morning I do remember having a hellava of a hangover.

To me it was becoming real that I was home and I began to loosen up and relax a bit. Of course I would see or hear things that would remind me of the miserable hell, the fear—of a combat infantryman, A DOUGHBOY.

THE END

RETROSPECT:
The First Twenty

Reminiscing is good for the character of a person and his soul.

As I became old enough to think and reason I became aware that I did not have things that other people around me had. I can't quite explain my feelings. As I got older I always hoped that the abundant life would come. I felt that I was a victim of poverty, yet I did not think about self pity. Nor did I realize or know that the way to a better life was knowledge.

As I went through life in the early forties, as a soldier, I began to have some of the good things that I thought made the abundant good life. Yet I complained, and griped, about my hard life as a soldier and trained very, very hard, to become a better one. I still considered myself in privation, yet still I did not think about self pity.

As I developed into a combat infantryman, starting with the invasion at Oran, Algeria. Then the Tunisian Campaign, the invasion and Campaign of Sicily, the invasion of Normandy, the Campaign of France, Belgium, and Germany; I began to realize that I had always had the abundant good life, compared to the tormenting hell, the misery, and—more hell as a combat infantryman, A DOUGHBOY.

My earlier complaining is like complaining about having no shoes and then seeing a man without feet.

I am very, very grateful and lucky, if there is such a thing as luck.

FINALE

CHAPTER TWELVE
Home and a Family

I had an awful hangover after a night of celebrating in the Big City (NY). Dreadfully forcing every move on the trip up to New Rochelle, it was a nice feeling to get off the noisy, jerky train. When I arrived at Jim's, I looked for a place to recoup. I was not much company to Rose and Jim for a while. Everyone was asking too many questions about things that I did not want to talk about. This was a problem with me for many months, for everyone wanted to talk about the war, and ask questions. My brother-in-law Willard Hassell, my sister Margie's husband, was the most inquisitive of all. He wanted to know about everything and continued to ask until he would wear me down. I told him things that I did not bother to tell others. We were very close. He was very proud of me, and Willard would brag to others about his brother-in-law's exploits. I would be self-conscious, embarrassed and somewhat uncomfortable at times. Willard sorta took the place of my many friends and buddies that I thought about often. Willard and I enjoyed our relationship very much. As I look back at the few people that influenced my life, Willard is one. After a day or two of recuperation, I was ready to visit the folks in South Alabama. Margie and Willard had taken care of Sandra, Jim and Rose's four year old daughter at times in the past when Rose was sick. They wanted me to bring Sandra to visit with them. I am not the type to mull over things, so it was a quick yes. Sandra was the first offspring of our clan of Spiveys, so she is special. I got Pullman tickets from New York to Montgomery. It was an uneventful trip as there were ma-mas always available when needed during times of minor crisis. Sandra was a good little traveler if she got what she wanted to eat, sweets.

The forty days or so that I was on leave with the folks was a whirlwind of activity. Much visiting, picnics, hay rides, juking and whatever event that popped up. Got acquainted with a few of the local young people and we chummed around a bit. About the only uncomfortable times was when Willard would brag on his brother-in-law. Though uncomfortable, I was sorta proud myself, and at times many over did the hero stuff. Until I sorta believed some of it and thinking maybe I was a bit of a brave warrior. They had no way of knowing of many, many times that I was frightened beyond comprehension. I had never given much thought as to my role in combat, and particularly whether I was a hero or not, my first need was to survive and go home. I know that combat is hell and that, is an understatement, and I did not want any more. All the folks, friends, and people I did not even know went all out to make my visit enjoyable. I went to Papa and Grandma's for a week or so and there was not much going on there. They lived out in the country about six miles from Atmore. Without a way to travel at Papa's it was sorta dull. Ray had left his thirty-six Ford car at Papa's, but it was worn out and not usable. The people and country had changed a lot in five years. All the young people I knew were off working or in the services. Most of our friends that Ray and I had gone hunting and fishing with before entering the service were scattered all over the country. So many were gone that I did not feel like I was home. Anyway the action place was at Margie and Willard's home in Andalusia. Willard kinda liked to juke and drink a beer occasionally. So did I. This got us in the doghouse occasionally.

All good things must end, so I returned by train to Fort Dix, a miserable trip that wore me out. I wished that I had gotten a reservation or Pullman ticket, for it seemed as if all servicemen were traveling. For about half the trip I did not have a seat. Arriving at Fort Dix, decision time came very quickly, whether to stay in or get out of the Army. Infantry NCO's that left Europe before I did and had reenlisted were on orders for Camp Stoneman, California. They were on their way to the war in the Pacific. Learning that, I made my decision very quickly, get the hell out. To me, going to the pacific was a cold ruthless stab, after three invasions, and seven campaigns, I repeat, I did not want any more combat. A veteran Infantry Major asked me if I wanted to stay in the Army, my answer was quick, "Hell no!"

The major, a bit perturbed, said, "Infantry NCO's don't usually talk to an officer like that."

Then I answered with a quick, "Hell no, Sir!"

I received my discharge 20 June 1945. My intentions had been to stay in the Army, had it not been for the possibility of assignment to the Pacific. Sergeant First Class was high on the totem pole in forty-five, there was only one higher Enlisted grade.

I wish I could remember what my possessions were when I left Ft. Dix. It certainly wasn't much. I remember that it was difficult to obtain civilian stuff. My civilian and extra military clothes and personal items I had left at my friends home, Paul Massian who lived in Auburn, Massachusetts when we shipped out of Fort Devens in forty-two. He was wounded in Africa and returned to the States. I did not locate him, so no junk. I visited a few others, only a few were home. I don't recall their names, but these visits brought back too many memories, so I went back to Jim and Rose's place at New Rochelle, then decision time again. After a day or two, I decided to stay with them, as jobs were more plentiful than in Alabama. The first job I tried was with Pepsi Cola as a route man. Not having any experience they put me with a fellow that was returning to work after being out sick for a few months, and he was not able to do much except drive and write out the sales slips. That meant I did all the hard work loading and unloading cases of Pepsi Cola into cellars and upstairs. I lasted one day. I then got a job in a factory that made freshwater purification kits (making drinking water from salt water). These kits were made for the Navy. I was classified as a defense worker, whoopee, big deal. This was a good job, no work, and in a few weeks I was promoted to an inspector, and all I did was look. This I was very well qualified to do, for that was about all I did was LOOK. All the employees were girls and women.

At this time mixing with people was not my strong point, I did not mix freely, didn't get acquainted with many people, I was somewhat a loner I guess. I would go to a movie and out to eat occasionally. At New Rochelle there was a very fine steak and fish restaurant, their specialty was lobster. That was it as for as my social life. With only a couple of acquaintances, the people or the area did not appeal to me. I just did not care much about making friends or whooping it up. A couple of times after a movie I would stop at a bar, have a drink; drinking alone was no fun, just plain dull without my buddies. I don't suppose that we WW11 Veterans made any connection between our feelings, our emotions or withdrawal from society.

After hearing of the dilemma of the Vietnam Veterans I feel that I can somewhat relate to their feelings and problems. All the combat veterans that I know, sucked it up and continued to adapt to the real life once more. We had been in many, many, shell shocking times and also feeling forsaken. What a difference maybe it would have made if everyone would have sucked it up and went on with their life as before the war, if possible. Sounds easy, huh?

Jim and Rose were making plans to go to Alabama to get Sandra, so I was considering returning to Alabama and live with Papa and Grandma at Atmore, or Margie and Willard at Andalusia. These were hard times for me, I was torn in several directions and unhappy. The worst part was I did not know what I wanted to do. No, the worst part is that I didn't know how to do anything, but to soldier. Lacking the knowledge to reason for a solution, as to the need for an education, training or vocation was beyond my capabilities. Anyway, my decision was to return to Alabama. Jim was the proud owner of an oil guzzling thirty-six Packard convertible that needed some attention, maybe an engine overhaul. It was decided that the least expensive way was just to put a couple of cans (large) of oil on the two rear step bumpers. That worked out just fine, and we laid a smoke screen all the way to Alabama. Another problem was, a Packard Sport Convertible seat is not very wide, and a very tight fit for three, and Sammy their ten months old son. Plus, Rose carries about everything that she thinks she might ever need. So there was no extra space at all. To try to beat the terrible driving conditions we left about eight at night. It was always a nerve wrecking experience to drive from New York through Washington. It was a good trip even with all the drawbacks. We stopped at Watkinsville, Georgia at Rose's Mother's home, she fed us the best country dinner ever. The trip and visiting are things that we still reminisce about and tell over and over.

Margie and Willard asked me to live with them, and I accepted. Desirable jobs were not so plentiful for an ex-soldier, especially for someone that could only march, fire mortars and machine guns. Willard was a route man with Coca Cola and didn't think that there was much future in that. So Willard, Wilbur my cousin, a very good mechanic, and I decided to start a business as partners. Willard knew of a small store for sale that had a full line of ration quotes (coupons) that went with the stock. It would take months plus to get coupons to stock rationed items for a new business. We were mostly interested in and needed the gas coupons, and the others, sugar, meat, cooking oil was a bonus. Buying the store was short a cut, it also meant that we would pay a premium for the stores stock (coupons).

We opened a combination garage, gas/service station, and with a small stock of fast-moving groceries. We did a lot of business, mostly on credit. I suppose all three partners were a soft touch as far as letting people have credit. If one had a good logical story it worked every time. Even though we had a large volume of business we were barely making a living. A six-day work week was the norm back then. I worked and studied hard to try to become a competent mechanic.

Late fall 1945 by chance all my brothers came at the same time, sorta a family reunion. My brother Roy served in the First Calvary Division in the Pacific. He had just got married to Emma Lee, a Texas girl, and they were going to make their home in West Texas at Big Spring. I had not seen Roy since fall 1936. Ray, served in the Navy; he had planned to make his home in California where he was starting to school, at the University of California at Berkley. I had not seen him since February 1940. Ray served on aircraft carriers first in the Atlantic and later in the Pacific during the war. Jim and family were on their way overseas, going to Japan. We had a lot of catching up to do. Getting reacquainted, telling war stories and drinking a little beer. It was happy times for us, we survived combat, and we knew we had been very, very, lucky indeed to have survived. We took Roy out one night and we forced down a few beers, the first mistake. We didn't bother calling and letting the wives know where we were; the second mistake, we got home after midnight, and were drunk. Third and fourth mistake. The fifth was making fun of the girls for being upset. We were in big trouble that lingered, and lingered, the wives have never put it to rest, but we can still laugh about it.

Spring of forty-six we leased a larger, better garage building with fine facilities for a garage and hired two mechanics. Even with this increase in business, the profit did not increase. Within a year the interests of Willard, Wilbur, and I began to go in different directions. Caused mainly by low income from the business. We sold the garage. Shortly afterwards Wilbur and I bought another business (we hadn't learned a thing about business and credit). This was a combination service station and groceries. It wasn't long before we saw that two families could not live on the profits. I bought Wilbur's share, I suppose I was determined to be a real dummy. I hadn't learned a thing. Later, December forty-seven a fellow made an offer to buy the business. With all the problems I was having with credit I didn't have to mull over it but for a short while. I received a cream puff 1940 Ford Deluxe, and a dab of cash for the service station. Reason for the description is that it was my first automobile, and I was proud of it. Automobiles were scarce and expensive. Forty Fords cost about six hundred dollars or a dab more new, and a cream-puff sold for about a thousand in forty-seven. This is the end of my business adventures. It is for sure that my adventures were nothing to brag about and certainly not any monetary gain.

Back tracking a bit, I met my sweetie and I married her, Euvida Castleberry, March 1946. A local girl from Red Level, Alabama. Marriage was great, but the meager earnings from the business did not provide much of a living for us. In fact, if it had been less we could not have even existed. I received twenty-seven dollars a month disability from the Government that was a help. One could rent a two-bedroom house for twenty-seven dollars or less in the late forties, or make a house payment. We did not have an automobile, very little furniture, no bank account, saying we were poor would be an understatement, but we felt secure. We did not have much fun time, where there were expenses involved, such as the movies, juking, travel, outside activities, nor did we do much visiting, for I worked seven days a week. Still all things considered, being newly married, knowing no better, we were more or less contented. Married life to me was not just a casual adventure, I took marriage seriously. We sorta believed that marriage was for a lifetime. I desperately wanted to provide more, particularly after the birth of Jimmy, our son. I was a very happy father, thankful and joyful to have a healthy, very handsome son. Jimmy changed all aspects of life for Beta and me. When it was just the two of us, we felt secure. It didn't mean the same as it did after Jimmy was born. We realized that we had to provide and plan for him at the present and for the future. We thought very much about our situation. Beta got a job around the end of 1947 or early 1948. It made life a little more comfortable for us. With Beta working to provide the grocery money we decided to build a home before I got a job. I started building and by the spring of 1948, I had it where we could move in, even though it was not completed. I built a five-room house for less than it would take to build a two-car garage now (ninety-three). We moved into our new home and I got a job as a carpenter's helper. I had interest in carpentry and liked the work. My first day I hauled fill dirt, loading and unloading by hand, a shovel that is, there wasn't much handy equipment around like we have now. The next morning it was the same thing, hauling dirt. At noon I asked, "What are we going to do this afternoon." The boss said, "Haul dirt." After digging holes from New England to Florida, Texas, Africa, and Europe, I had sworn many times while digging foxholes in the Army, that I was not going to make a living moving dirt, I quit promptly.

After the dirt hauling job, summer of forty-eight, I started working in a garage for twenty-five dollars a week (six day weeks) with a promise of a substantial raise, or work on commission, that never came.

After about two months I quit, went to work as a laundry/dry cleaning route man. That had good promise, but that did not work either. I was assigned the Elgin Air Force Base route that had a large volume of business. The Air Force at that time was really moving people around. I would get a good customer and all of a sudden, they would move leaving a laundry and dry-cleaning bill, and that loss was mine. What hurt most was the arrangement made by the owner. I was to deliver dry cleaning and laundry to unit supply rooms at Elgin Field. They were supposed to collect as it was picked up, but they did not. The owner was supposed to correct this give away. Some weeks I would work for particularly nothing. On top of that, I worked twelve to fifteen hours a day, six days a week. November and December of fortyeight, I did not have money to buy tags for the car (1940 Ford). Which cost about seven dollars. Neither did I have money to buy Christmas things. However, I did manage to buy Beta a ball point pen, that cost a dollar, and was one of the most sought after items at that time. If it had not been for Beta's pay check we would not have eaten. My spirits were way, way down, unable to give Beta and Jimmy just a few of the good things of life was horrible for me. I started looking for another line of work. One of the big drawbacks when job hunting was that I was a veteran and could draw money from the government (GI Bill), called on the job training. No one, I mean no one would pay decent wages; they wanted one to work for them and let the government pay. It was easy to get work when the employer knew that one was a veteran and could get paid by the Government's GI Bill.

The owner of Plymouth/ Chrysler wanted to hire me, said that he had heard that I was a good mechanic. As my hopes leaped, I asked him, "How much do you pay a mechanic?" I had heard that he paid above average. His answer was, "well lets see, you are a veteran, the Government will pay you a hundred twenty, I will pay you fifteen a week, that makes forty-five a week, that's good wages." That almost pulled my trigger. My answer was, "Mr. Merrill, I won't be working for the Government, and I think you should pay me, not the Government. You can take that fifteen dollars and shove it up your... , where the sun don't shine." I finally went to the Army Recruiting Office and found out that I could enlist, as a Sergeant First Class. I didn't take them up on it right then, this was the week after Christmas. After a few trips on the route working my butt off, twelve to fifteen hours a day, I was just about fed up. So on the 4th of January forty-nine, I went to work as usual about six a.m.. By nine a.m., my helper and I finished loading the truck and trailer, just packed full, and started for the Elgin Field area. As I was driving, I was thinking about how hard I was working and the meager wages I was receiving, some weeks none. As I stopped at a red light in Crestview, Florida and on the spur of the moment, I applied the parking brakes, looked over at my helper, opening the door at the same time and said, "Take this load and deliver it, or do whatever you want to do and when you get back, tell the boss I quit."

I hitched-hiked back to Andalusia, went by the Army Recruiting Office and reenlisted in the Army. I was to leave in a couple hours for Ft. Jackson, South Carolina. I went home for a few minutes to bid Beta and Jimmy goodbye, and promised to return as soon as I could. The car did not have the new tags for 1949, nor did I have money to buy them, so I had to go to Fort Jackson by bus. The first payday I returned home, I loaded everything we could get into the car and returned to Fort Benning, and Beta and Jimmy started their Army career. Dependents have to put up with all the Army crap just like everyone else. Dependents have Army careers too as far as I'm concerned.

A Doughboys Narrative   ●

CHAPTER THIRTEEN
Starting Over

At Ft. Jackson, the same old processing of aptitude tests, getting your basic issue of clothing and then assignment, which was Ft. Benning, Georgia. It took about ten days or so for all this and then I went to Ft. Benning for my second Army career. The Army was reactivating the Third Division then and was in desperate need of bodies. I did not want to go back into the Infantry. I was still having a little leg trouble (War wounds), so I went to the 703rd Ordnance Company to ask about a position (job). They must have liked what they heard, for right away, I was assigned to the 703rd Ordnance Company as Platoon Sergeant, and shop foreman within a few weeks, this was a Master Sergeant's job and position. Can you image an infantry platoon sergeant being given a job such as this without ordnance experience. The Company had a surplus of Master Sergeants, and they were supposed to be assigned as Platoon Sergeants and/or Shop Foremen. I was only a Sergeant First Class. I held this position until November 1951 when I left Korea, plus being the NCOIC of the forward Ordnance Detachment. I was promoted to Master Sergeant earlier in fifty-one.

I must back track a bit to try to explain the changes, etc., of the World War II Army and the Army of forty-nine. It was no problem to get back to soldiering. I knew how to soldier, and above all, I wanted to be a good soldier; that was my goal when I enlisted in 1940. What I noticed most was the indifferent attitude in discipline, respect, and expertise of the duties to be performed. We had so many that didn't care, had no desire, they tried very hard to get a section 8 or undesirable discharge. In just three and a half years there had been drastic changes. These plus bad conduct discharges were given frequently in an effort to weed out the duds. During the war years and before, orders and instructions were to be followed as soon as possible, with no delay or contentious questions. We had a lot of problems with that, for my expectation of obedience was always high. I was known as a chicken s... SOB by some, but fair, and most of my men respected me, there were more men trying to get into the platoon than there were trying to get out.

Beta and I had a rough time trying to make ends meet during the past couple years. The regular pay check was great, and by giving attention to how we spent our earnings, we began to live very well on my Army pay. Jim was stationed at Ft. Benning and we rented a house that was large enough for both families in Columbus. This arrangement lasted until he was assigned to Okinawa.

I will mention just a little about my fifteen or so years of Army life of forty-nine to sixty-five. Hoping to show my love and dedication to the Army and my Country. It is hard for me to write about myself; even if this Narrative is mostly about me, and maybe some will think that I am bragging. I try very hard to keep me out of this Narrative as a braggadocio. It is WE, that accomplished so much, and WE, were proud of our exploits. For a start I will say this; my efficiency always put me in the top 10 percent as to soldiering, supervision, responsibilities, proficiency and ability. I tried and believed that I was a good soldier and a Non Commissioned Officer, always willingly accepted responsibility and got the job done. I always had good relationships with most enlisted men and in good rapport with most officers. My advancement in the Army was accomplished by performance and being in the right place at the right time, not brown nosing, nor was I a yes man. I had awards for bravery and the Combat Infantryman Badge, various letters for excellent performance. As a recipient of these awards, and wearing the RED ONE, I received a bit of respect, kinda like the E.F. Hutton commercial, (when they speak, people listen). I tried to be a good soldier and being an NCO during all my combat time, meant that when I spoke, most soldiers paid attention. My performance and conduct were governed by Army Regulations. In just about all my assignments locations and job responsibilities I was contented, with only a couple exceptions. Enough smoke, so I will continue.

Soldiering in forty-nine and fifty was rather difficult for the following reasons. There were quite a few men in the Army that did not like Army life, did not want to soldier, nor do anything else that should have been normal. Some were very good at giving NCOs a hard time, requiring constant supervision. My background of the War years and earlier was that an NCO took care of most problems. The Army was not a place for crybabies, if there was a problem, "take care of it"; good officers backed the good NCO 100%. The changing Army made this almost impossible to take care of problems on your own. The Army started leaning toward the misfits, (feeling that they were mistreated, and needed protection). NCOs and officers hands were tied to some extent. In some instances some commanders and officers were reluctant to give punishment to offenders because of fear it would be a bad reflection on their (officers and NCO's) ability. And maybe in some cases this was true. In the Army just about everyone wanted advancement, amazing to me only a few wanted responsibilities. Many officers feared making decisions without checking it out from higher up. It could have been they didn't know, or want to. Anyway we had our share off duds, EM and officers. I was overruled a few times on punishment that I imposed on some of the misfits. When guys would screw up, I would LET them clean the latrines in the evenings, during their off duty times, police up the area and such. Another example, if any of my men did not clean his weapon properly, or pass inspection, I would detail them, on their own time, to clean the platoon's crews served weapons (fifty caliber machine guns). As time progressed, these petty punishments became unpopular and overruled by the Brass. I was considered by these men (misfits), as CS SOB and disliked, while most respected me and considered me just a GI SOB. I considered myself a performer, getting the job done. I knew how to soldier, and did soldier; always trying to do my best and expected no less from others, I am not or was I ever by any means, perfect. I was probably disliked (or hated) for the misery I caused for the misfits. Always pushing them to the limit, do it right and do it now, the misfits of the day did not like that type of soldiering, all they wanted was to get out of the Army.

As I look back, it seems improbable or impossible that I made the transition from a Doughboy to an Ordnance Shop Foreman/Platoon Sergeant with the amount of success (I am not bragging) that I did. I give all the credit to my Infantry training and experience, that enabled me to lead, persuade, or do whatever, to influence men to do the job.

At Ft. Benning, we always had more work than we could do, plus some training. Just about always the Ordnance Unit was expected to do the impossible, that is do all the maintenance without any backup support, plus all the CS training, some needed it, a few didn't. These expectations meant that we had a seven day work week most of the time. My special assignments were icing on the cake, the last two assignments, Panama and Fort McPherson were tops and very rewarding and blissful. Late winter of 1950, we went for amphibious training at Norfolk, then on to Viegas, Puerto Rico for amphibious operations. While at Camp Picket at Blackstone, Va. Beta and Jimmy came up for a couple of weeks. From there I went to Puerto Rico. We made a Port call at Port au Prince, Haiti. I was detailed (I sorta volunteered) as the NCOIC of the Shore Courtesy Patrol (MP). By this time most knew that if I was given a job I would do it, and try to do it the GI way. For these reasons The Ordnance Officer and the CO put me in charge. Everyone enjoyed their visit, without any major incidents. Other than being away from the family a few weeks, it was a good trip.

In July 1950, I put in for a maintenance school and was accepted and after attending two months I was taken out of school in August when the Division was sent to Korea via Japan. We processed and loaded all our equipment and supplies for points west for shipment to Japan and Korea. These were sad times for thousands of families as we departed Ft.Benning. It was much more regrettable and heart wrenching leaving a family than it was back in 1942. Then it was also a certain amount of adventure to look forward to. Other than the few weeks I was on the Puerto Rico trip we were together as family. These were enjoyable times. After our year and a half at Ft. Benning's good duty and we dreaded being separated. I was in Korea sixteen months, that seemed like a life time. We still had the forty Ford and while I was in Korea we started saving to buy a new Crown Victoria Ford that we both liked. During this time Beta learned how to drive. She imposed upon herself the task to start the car to keep the battery charged, that led to moving it back and forth, then driving on the street. When I returned, Beta had her driver's license.

We departed for San Francisco in August fifty and arrived in Saesabo, Japan in September. We set up camp in tents up in the mountains at an Army maneuver area on the Southern Island of Kyushu. Japan was much different from other places I had been, and a beautiful country. Other than a storm with torrential rains for a couple days the weather was great. I experienced my first earthquake and it were a weird feeling. And in the cities particularly, it was a solid mass of people, I don't think that I could ever learn to like being in such crowds.

Shortly after arriving in Japan our Company received one hundred sixty South Korean civilians to train and make soldiers out of them. It was odd or cruel the way South Korea "drafted" men for army service. I was told that the Military Police would drive around over town looking for draft age men. When they saw a man that looked suitable for the army, they loaded him into the truck. At that moment they were in the army, some said that the draftees were not even given the opportunity to bid farewell to their family. The Company Commander detailed me to train these men. Our task was to give the Koreans their basic military training (School of a Soldier) and later they would be given on the job training for mechanics and ordnance supply technicians. I was the only senior ex-infantry Non Commissioned Officer in the Company, therefore I was detailed for the job of supervising the Korean's military training. The Brass was kind enough to let me pick four NCO's from the company to assist me. We had only four weeks to do the job. None of us could speak Korean, so all commands were given in English.

After four weeks the Korean's could drill, manual of arms using English commands; and extended order drill by following arm and hand signals. We had accomplished our mission, I thought very well. The brass thought we did well too by giving us letters of appreciation. The ROKS (Republic of Korea Soldiers) acted as if they appreciated our efforts teaching then how to soldier and prepare them to be able to defend their Country. The Koreans were very dedicated, ingenious, and good workers; we trained the Koreans to be competent mechanics and supply technicians. It was a challenge and extremely rewarding.

The nearest town was down the mountain about six miles. While we were there, a storm hit the Island with heavy, heavy rain. The night of the raging storm, the duty NCO woke me and informed me that the MP's had two of my men (one US soldier one ROKS), and the CO wanted me to go get them. Needless to say that I was really teed off. Anyone that caused such misery to a person on a night like we were having, deserved the worst. I went to the MP office and signed for them and went out to the jeep. As they started to get in, I said, "Hold it, hold it, get in front of this jeep, and if you don't walk, I will run over you." Now they were mad, they walked all the way up the mountain to our camp, about six miles. The rain storm never let up. Walking speed was about as fast as one could drive in the down pour. We got back to camp about five a.m., the two men were soaking wet, a bit tired, hung over and were ready for sack time, and angry. I got them a couple of picks and shovels and marked a six foot square (it was still raining); and ordered the men, to dig! Now they had something to be angry about. When breakfast came, I gave them time to eat, then more digging. By that afternoon they had dug a mighty fine hole, six by six. That was the last time that anyone from our Company tried to slip into town. We called punishment such as this, making'em or breaking'em, making them sorry they screwed up, breaking them from wanting to do it again.

In October, we went to Beppue for a couple of weeks then we boarded the ship for Wonsan, North Korea. As we left Japan and the nearer we got to N.Korea the colder it got. I don't think I got warm until the next spring. Arriving in Wonsan, the First Platoon was designated the Forward Support Detachment. We left the Company and moved inland to join the 65th Infantry RCT (Regimental Combat Team), to give them Ordnance support. We were about sixty miles northwest of Wonsan toward the Chinese Border. In a short while, a week or so, the Chinese invited themselves into the fight. The Chinese had been in it for a while, but it wasn't common knowledge. The 65th RCT and the Ordnance Detachment had to make a rapid withdrawal. We left some equipment. Returning to Wonsan, it was a race against time and the Chinese to get our remaining equipment loaded before the Chinese closed in on Wonsan. Our Detachment was able to get most of our equipment and supplies out. What we couldn't take out, we burned. We returned to Pusan and camped about 30 miles northwest of Pusan, to wait for our equipment. As the equipment and supplies came in we would sort it out and try to see that it got to the right people and place. We lucked up and found a box of ten shotguns. We very quickly liberated the shotguns and put them on our supply truck. We had been seeing pheasants and could not resist taking the shotguns. As soon as we could, we started hunting pheasants. They were mighty fine eating. The Division Supply Officer learned after about four months that we were hunting with shotguns and he also knew he was missing a case. He put out the word that he would sure like to find ten shotguns. We got the message and made sure that he found ten shotguns.

With some confusion, some disappointment about having to withdraw, our moral was not of the highest level. We should have learned a lot from the Korean chaos, but from some of the predicaments we have gotten into since I don't think we learned much.

One of the most terrible events of my career happened at this time when we were low anyway. We got a beer ration and some of the men got drunk and started shooting their weapons. I sent the Duty NCO to stop it. By the time he got back they had started shooting again. The Duty NCO and I returned to the tent that was doing most of the firing (shooting). I told them to stop it and I got lip. Then I proceeded taking their weapons. I had collected a few weapons when three or four jumped me, one of our men was hit in the head by a slug from a forty-five-caliber pistol, he was very seriously wounded. The results was an investigation, people were charged, some were convicted. One of the big problems in the investigation was the shot fired was from one of the pistols that I had appropriated. No one knew who fired the shot. I was under investigation and relieved of duties for a couple of weeks before everything was over. Some of the guys said I was the one that fired the pistol that wounded the soldier. It wasn't proved who fired the shot that seriously wounded one of our men. There was much trouble and chaos that night, that left bad feelings among some of the troops. It was devastating to all of us. I thought then, and still think that it is unwise to supply troops acholic beverages.

As soon as the Division received their equipment, or most of it, and we got organized, they moved the Division to the front and of course the Detachment went up also. I lost all my extra clothes that were in a trailer. Starting in January 1951 and continuing until I left Korea, it was push and/or withdraw, some by choice, and some by the so called "cease fire terms" about all the time, attacking here and there or defending. Rumors and more rumors of a cease fire or whatever, it wasn't an ideal situation for soldiers that were trained to destroy and win. While in

Korea it was my job to set our defensive perimeter around the Company. Some units were just about wiped out by infiltrators and guerrillas. We were lucky, we were never attacked directly. They were in our area a few times but did not make an attack. Being in a support unit was a vacation compared to what the Doughboys were doing.

The last of October fifty-one, I was selected to rotate back to the states. The rotation system was slow to start, many rumors but not anyone departing. The excuse was that there were not sufficient replacements coming in. Our counter argument was if General MacAurther could be shanghaied, fired, relieved or whatever, then why couldn't we go home. Most of us thought that if McAurther was expendable, everyone was expendable. Some of us did not like the way Truman handled the situation, nor the actions or lack of by the Military Staff in the Pentagon. In November I was selected to rotate home. I wanted to return to my family, but I had many good friends that I hated to leave. Including were many Koreans that I had trained that by now were excellence soldiers, mechanics, and supply technicians. In Japan I had a delay of about a week. I had been recommended to be commissioned a Warrant Officer and I would have to stay in Korea if I were to be Commissioned. I declined, and by that I was allowed to rotate home. On the voyage to Seattle, we were treated to a Thanksgiving Dinner. When we arrived at Ft. Lawton, at Seattle, we were treated to another Thanksgiving Dinner and as always Army Thanksgiving and Christmas Dinners are memorable occasions. Late at night we boarded a train, Pullman accommodations, our destination, Ft. Jackson, South Carolina. And would you believe that we were treated to another Thanksgiving Dinner, thanks to the Great Northern Railroad, the dinner was very good and paid for by the Army. All things considered, it was a good trip, just slow for we were in a big hurry to get home. It probably took five to six weeks to make the trip; now the trip is measured in hours. Being a transit is a most undesired situation Army wide, check this, check that, fill out meaningless forms, on and on. It seems that just about always something is screwed up or missing, very serious predicaments if one is in a hurry. Yet, sometimes it is so screwed up that it is comical.

Arriving home, the first order of business was getting reacquainted, and visiting relatives and friends until the first week of January. And of course we looked for that Crown Victoria Ford, that we had been dreaming about. We couldn't find one, we settled for a 1951 Ford Deluxe two door. I did not like it as well as the old one, even though it was probably a better car. Beta and Jimmy went with me to Ft. Jackson as I waited for assignment orders. We were there for about a month and received orders for Ft. Chaffee, Arkansas. The rat race starts. We moved six times and were assigned to five different Army Post, in fifty-two. One won't accumulate much junk moving. This was normal in my Army career, moving. In my almost twenty-two years I was stationed at nineteen different Army Posts. This doesn't include Europe, Africa, the Far East, Middle East and Honduras. And would you believe that I was on seventeen different Ships, going to and from overseas and amphibious maneuvers and combat beach assaults. This does not include an LSI and an LST voyage from England to France, and two sea going ferry crossings between Japan and Korea.

We put everything that we could get into the car thinking that Ft. Chaffee would be our new duty station. It was not, we still had a way to go. While at Chaffee waiting for orders we ran out of money. Back then while in transit one hardly ever got paid. I could not get a check cashed and as we left for Ft. Polk I had to get advance travel pay to make the trip. After all these problems of not having any money and skimping on everything, when we arrived at Polk as we unpacked, we discovered in our luggage our War Bonds. Sometimes one is just eat up with the dumb A.., this is an example of CRS at a young age. At Ft. Polk, Louisiana, I was assigned to the 737th Ordnance. They in turn gave me the job as the Chief Inspector. I didn't last long at this job, I suppose that I was a bit too GI for the National Guard Unit that had been just called to activate duty.

Another thing that was very noticeable that Regular Army NCO's were not assigned to positions with a lot of responsibilities. The 737th was sorta disorganized and lacking a bit in expertise. Also, the Division was strong on chicken s... petty SOP's (Standing Operating Procedure); such as all personnel had to stay on post two nights a week (Tuesday, Thursday). It was very few of the National Guard that had their dependents in the area. We, the Regular Army felt it was a slap toward us. Me being away from the family for seventeen months, I didn't like that at all. Reveille daily at 0600, the nearest housing we could find was fifty-five miles from Polk. I took a few days leave to look for a house trailer. Found one we liked I moved into a trailer park just out side the main gate at Polk. Less than ten minutes from work, I never liked long traveling time to and from work. Also I think maybe the National Guard fellows had a grudge against us, The Regular Army. This feeling might have been mutual, we Korean Veterans were sorta cocky and held the Guard in low esteem anyway I guess. I was transferred to The Division Tank Battalion. I had no job or responsibilities there and was dissatisfied. I considered myself sorta a go getter and used to being in the position of making things happen. Army Field Forces sent an Inspection Team to check on the Division's readiness. I was at the motor pool doing nothing when the Team arrived, and in the Team was an Ordnance Colonel I knew while in the 3rd Division at Ft. Benning and Korea. When he saw me, he started toward me and me to him. As I approached, his words were,

"What in the hell are you doing here?" I told him I had no job and all about being shanghaied out of Ordnance. I told all this in the presence of the Division and Tank Battalion Officers, they didn't like what I was saying, the truth hurts. When I had finished, the Colonel said, "When I get to Ft. Sam Houston, (Fourth Army Headquarters), I will straighten this out and you will have a job." Within a week, I had orders for Ft. Hood and the 2nd Armored Division Ordnance Battalion. My opinion of Ft. Hood and Ordnance shop operations was about the same as they were at Ft. Polk, a lot to be desired. I stayed there until June and was discharged. I didn't care much for Ft. Hood, so I went back to Ft. Benning and reenlisted in the 30th Infantry Tank Co. as Motor Sergeant. The company ran the tank tactics demonstrations problems for the Infantry School. I was there as Motor Sergeant for seven months and the Company passed their first Command Maintenance Inspection in four years. I suppose that is the reason that the Company Commander told everyone I was in charge of the Company Maintenance Program, and no one would interfere and follow maintenance instructions. I had an Ordnance MOS (Military Occupation Specialty) and was in a different job so the Army began trying to put me back into Ordnance, so I volunteered for assignment to Iran as an Ordnance Maintenance and Supply advisor. My seven months at Ft. Benning was routine. Beta, Jimmy, and I loved Ft Benning and had many good times there. It was a busy place for us, visiting, keeping up with local happenings kept us on the go. Assignments like this one are periods of good times that sorta makes up for the miserable.

A Doughboys Narrative ●

CHAPTER FOURTEEN
More Adventure and The Good Years

I arrived in Iran in February fifty-two, now that assignment certainly was not routine like Ft. Benning. It took a few days for briefings, and the getting necessary equipment then on to Isfahan. I enjoyed the year in Isfahan, Iran, but it was horrible being away from the family. Beta and Jimmy were supposed to have joined me in Teheran, that was canceled after I arrived in Iran. Disappointment is not the right word. I was an advisor to the Ninth Iranian Infantry Division and accomplished very little while there, certainly nothing to brag about. It was quite amusing at times. Like when the Division returned from a training exercise and had left their vehicles scattered around with flat tires, wouldn't run and such. Next door was the horse/mule artillery units that were busy taking care of their horses and I pointed out to the Commander that one vehicle could carry much more than many mules, and that the vehicles were worthless if they didn't operate. He understood my point, but it didn't change things much. Then I could look around me and see buildings, bridges, and their wells and water systems and such that had been in use for centuries. An arched bridge that crossed the river at Isfahan that was constructed six centuries ago. Constructed with sun dried mud bricks and rocks, still standing, Who's the dummy?

Isfahan at one time was the capital of Persia. There were places of interest in Isfahan, the markets, Mosques, and the old Place, and gardens. Nearby was located the old, old capital of Persia, Persepeles. A lot of historical places, things of interest and I did quite a bit of looking. If I had known more about world history then, I would have enjoyed it much more. Duty hours of the Iranian Army were eight to two in winter and seven to one in summer. A lot of idle hours. I was near Persepeles a couple of times while hunting; and have regretted not making a tour of the old city. One of the most interesting things was the camel caravans arriving and departing for places many days out into the boondocks. In winter when they would go high up into the mountains where it was very cold; to keep the baby camels from freezing they would fasten blankets on them. The drivers made their seat or "nest" as comfortable as possible and took turns sleeping on the journey. Much of the traveling was at night. There are many stories about the camel drivers going to sleep, waking up lost or many miles off track.

I became friends with a few Iranians and went hunting a number of times and enjoyed cook-outs on these hunting trips. The hunting trips were mostly day affairs and when/or if we killed a gazelle they would dress it out, find shade under a cliff, trees were few, in most areas where we hunted there were none. They prepared lunch and we would have gazelle on a stick, flat bread, and tea. Don't knock it, it is finger licking good. Especially after many hours chasing gazelles across the valleys and up into the hills. I learned that a gazelle can run faster than a jeep, cross country. Tea time took precedent over everything else, served in small cups and lumps of hard sugar. One would put a lump of hard sugar in your mouth, sip a bit of tea, until it got sweet enough and swallow. Drinking tea over there, was an art. I also went on three hunting trips for a few days, to two different friends home, ranch/farm, that were sixty miles or so from Isfahan. There would be rooms with clean straw, this was the sleeping room; Another large room with pillows, back rests, with rugs on the tile floor. One night we had gazelle stew with vegetables and bread, the bread was about as large as a dinner plate and just as thin or thinner, no plates nor utensils. One would take the flat bread, tear off a piece, fold in such a way to dip up the stew to your mouth. With about eight people dipping out of the same pot, makes it a prolonged occasion, I think occasion is the right word. The only thing that could have improved this eating is a spoon. On these occasions there would be an opium puffer or two. They would move away from the group with their opium, pipes and glowing pieces of charcoal, puff, and get high. The others didn't seem to notice, or think anything out of the ordinary about it. Of course the people and their life style was very strange, odd, different or whatever. Other than the fanatics' one could get acquainted. To a fanatic Moslem all Christians or non Moslem are inferior and unclean. Some will not use things touched by a none Moslem. About once a month it was customary to be invited to tea by the officers that I had contact with or were supposed to be advising. At the tea the host, a male servant, my interpreter and I were the only ones seen, it was not a family thing. I never met any of their family. Just as well, because with the language barrier, background, culture, idle conversation is very difficult.

As my date for returning to the States drew nearer I got more anxious every day. Iran would have been a good tour if only Beta and Jimmy could have been with me. Without them it had been dreadful and now I was going home. Traveling in the early fifty's compared to now was primitive. It took three days to get to Tripoli, close to a week wait there, and almost four days from Tripoli to Westover AFB, Massachusetts with stops at Casablanca, Azores, Bermuda and then a long three days to Andalusia, Alabama, including a quick stop in Washington. After a few days at home, I got word that I would go to the Army Language School at Monterey, California in July. Results of my stop in Washington. That meant I would have to find something to do at Ft. Jackson for a few months. This was a dreadful predicament to be in, as a transit in a Replacement Company you are just a body. Apt to be doing most anything, in charge of petty details with men that are just passing through and didn't want to do anything and not overly cooperative. A very undesirable position to be in and especially for a few months. After about a week, I was ready to do most anything. At the morning and afternoon formations for roll call some of the time there would be guys horsing around in ranks, not paying attention to roll call or anything else. This particular morning, I got the First Sergeant's attention and asked him to hold everything for a moment. I went back into ranks and started telling the guys that were horsing around to fall out to the rear. After getting most of the offenders in a group in rear of the formation I proceeded telling this group what was expected of soldiers, and what would happen if they did not act like one. That was the end of the disturbances. After the formation, the First Sergeant asked me to assist him in conducting the roll calls and detail assignments, I attended two formations a day, but that wasn't enough for me, doing nothing is worse than working. After a few weeks, I asked and received temporary assignment to the Ft. Jackson Ordnance Office. I worked there until I left in June for The Army Language School, Monterey, California.

In June we sold our house trailer that we had bought while we were at Fort Polk. Jam packed as much as we possibly could into the fifty-one Ford, it's hard to believe that we could put just about all we had into a fifty-one Ford. If we moved now it would take an eighteen wheeler. We took off for Andalusia for a few days and then, points west. We visited along the way with family and did much sight seeing. The trip across the Southwest was hot. Not many or any cars were equipped with air conditioning in the early fifties. My Uncle Benny gave me a water evaporation type air conditioner. It helped in the desert heat, we had to put water in it frequently, a few times I would put too much in it. A slight swerve and Beta would get a bath. That almost cost me a plumb good wife. I was proud of the fifty-one Ford, it performed faultless in the scorching heat of the SW. Arriving in Monterey, we were lightly dressed and almost froze before we could dig out more clothes. A change from a hundred degrees plus weather to the forties is noticeable.

I started classes at the Language School to learn Spanish. I did not know English grammar and learning another language was a bit rough, I was ranked twenty out of a class of twenty-two, wasn't many between me and the bottom. We loved Monterey and would have liked another tour in that area, but never did, and now I wouldn't even think of going there, too crowded. We did some sight seeing, went to the California State Fair which was very, very good. We visited my brother, Ray and family at Redding, we saw a bit of California in these few months. We had to delay our departure waiting for the birth of our second child. In January our daughter arrived, we were more than proud and happy for our beautiful, healthy, daughter. After a month delay we hit the road for Andalusia, Alabama. We traded for a Chevy station wagon, with standard transmission which we were advised would be better in the mountains of Honduras. It wasn't, a couple of times we had to push a bit in some of the mountains. This Chevy was about the most unresponsive automobile that I ever owned. After visiting a few days, then on to New Orleans, with stops in Merida, Mexico, San Salvador, and finally arrived at Tegucigalpa Honduras in February fifty-four. This was to be our home for about three years.

Conditions in Honduras were a bit primitive, for getting things needed for the children. Schools left much to be desired, the right foods, such as milk and vegetables were lacking. We liked Honduras and made many friends. We met a couple and their son from Mississippi, they were in the lumber business in a big way. We would go out into the boondocks on weekends to their sawmill and explore the area. With the family, we toured El Salvador, Guatemala and Panama. With the exception of Copan and the Northeast Coast, I did a lot of traveling around over the country. I went on a couple of duck hunting trips to the South Coast; that was a great experience. Plus we hunted ducks and game birds locally. I suppose one of the most enjoyable was the close relationships among the Mission personnel. We worked very hard at trying to stay busy and not get into idle ruts of doing nothing and drinking. We were there during a couple of minor revolutions. (For those that were wounded and killed it was not minor). These were a little nerve wracking, concern for the families was great. Our biggest problem while there was that Jimmy could not adapt to the school. We sent Jimmy back to the States early to live with my brother at Redding Ca. So that he could settle in to the US school system and schedule. To give some idea as what I thought about Honduras (the Government) is what I would say to my Honduran friends in our bull sessions and kidding. I would tell them that I had rather be a Master Sergeant in the United States Army, than to be the President of Honduras. They would get a kick out of that one. It also indicates our good relationship, and job wise, I think also it would apply to much of the world. I have always hoped to return to Honduras but now after all these years it would not be the same.

In the fall of fifty-seven, we started planning our trip back to the states and that was to drive back. So here it is. We left Tegucigalpa, driving a Fifty-two-Mercury Monterey by way of El Salvador, Guatemala, Mexico, entering the States at Laredo, Tx. We had already made a visit to El Salvador and Guatemala. So we did not do much sight seeing until we got into Mexico. We arrived in Tapachula, Mexico at ten or eleven at night after some delay at the entry point into Mexico. They claimed that the border was closed and would not open until eight the next morning. I had to make a little payment before they would let us cross. Got a place to stay and then I loaded the car on the train that was to leave the next morning for Arriaga, Mexico. About an eight-hour trip. By way of the Pan American Highway through Mexico on to Laredo, Texas. We did a lot of looking and picture taking.

We stayed at Oaxaca a couple of days, visiting some very historical and interesting places, the cities of Oaxaca and Monte Alban were impressive. On to Mexico City for few days, where we did a lot of looking in and around Mexico City. One the most interesting was the celebration at the Shrine of the Virgin of Guadalupe. The markets in Mexico City were remarkable, most any goody imaginable could be purchased. I have always wanted to go back to Central America for an extended visit, particularly Mexico and Guatemala. How can I say that, for in reality all Central America and South America is a dream place to visit. There are untold numbers of beautiful, interesting and historical things that could and would be exciting and enjoyable.

Someday I hope to go back. I must say, though, as we crossed the Rio Grand into Texas and the USA, we breathed a sigh of relief. It was nice to be back. At times I sorta think that this great country of ours would be much better if; everyone spent time in a foreign country. It would probably help us be better citizens; then I see and hear some travelers, particular the bleeding heart liberal media crowd and educators, that are travelers, then I think maybe we would be better if... Jimmy was staying with my brother, Ray, at Redding, California, and we were anxious to see him. We spent a of couple days with my brother, Roy, at Big Spring, TX. Left there for Victorville, California and spent a night with Beta's sister. We did not make long visits for we were sorta in a hurry, the closer we got. It seems that on every move for some reason, it is always, rush, rush, rush. We ran into a sand storm in Southern California that ruined the windshield, the lights, and paint on the front of the car. We were in a predicament where we did want to stop. The sand starting blowing all of a sudden, there was no advantage in turning around or parking beside the road. I knew that the sand (rocks) was doing extensive damage. So Sele-Gere.

Finally, arriving at my brother's and being with Jimmy was much joy. It was also nice to know that we were able to relax after more than two weeks on the road. We went to Ft. Lewis Washington around the first of January fifty-eight to get Jimmy in school and find a place to live. Houses were very expensive, and not many were available so we bought a house trailer. I never did learn to like house trailer living. By living in a trailer, I was just five to ten minutes from the barracks, which was great. I was assigned to A Company 704th Ordnance Battalion.

I spent almost two miserable years with A Company. Miserable in that we were continually working, training and more training. With all the training we did it was still expected that we do all the maintenance that was required. Again, needless to say that seven-day work week was the norm. We were either going out in the field, maneuvers or getting ready to go. The 4th Division, a STRAC (or whatever) division, and I don't think that we ever got as good as we were supposed to be, for we trained, practiced, and had dry runs continually. Every year we would go to Yakima for maneuvers. And just to think that orders assigning me to the School of Americas at Fort Gulick, Canal Zone was pigeonholed for about three months. I wanted to get out of the 4th Division bad, and it really teed me off. It seems that they wanted me to make the trip to California before I went to Panama. At certain times of the year parts of Washington is an ideal area for extremes, if one has to be out in the boondocks. It is either too hot or too cold, muddy or dusty, too wet or too dry, not a good place to play in the woods or desert at certain times of the year. The Division went on amphibious maneuvers in the fall of fifty-eight to Moro Bay, California and the Ordnance Battalion sent a small group to support them. If you recall, the chapter telling about Sicily, is titled, Getting Good, You Pay the Price. I felt the same way on this operation. In a small group in order to give sufficient support, all personnel had to be the best available. Who did they select to go? Me, as the NCOIC. I was sorta perturbed again. But if it hadn't been for being away from the family, it would have been great. We went to Moro Bay by motor convoy and returned to Seattle on a ship. The weather was good by West Coast standards and when we returned to Ft. Lewis, snow was on the ground.

Summer of fifty-eight, I took a thirty-day leave and drove back to Alabama and Georgia and took a different route each way. We visited Yellowstone for a couple of days, and it is a sight worth seeing, in eighty-six we visited again for a few days. What a change, Yellowstone is becoming a tinsel town. We did some traveling around in Washington and I would have done more if I could have had more off duty time. Did a lot of fishing and some camping, (sorta roughing it, tents and gas stoves). As a lover of the outdoors, I loved Washington, and Washington is one of the most beautiful states. A great thing happened while at Ft. Lewis, and that was the birth of one more healthy, beautiful, daughter. We were overjoyed with her arrival, and my children, are my greatest joy. They are still, and the icing on the cake is the four grandchildren. They are the joy of my life, what a great gift. We traveled across country with Cathy when she was three weeks old. Across country again with Debbie who was about seven months old. We learned that it is a pain to travel with babies.

I had about a seven-day notice to get ready to ship out for the Panama Canal Zone. I flooded the neighborhood with fish, rainbow trout, cod and salmon. I was not able to sell my trailer in such short notice, nor boat. I must mention one of the delicacies of Washington, that is kippered salmon, I can eat it like cake. I left the trailer to be sold by a dealer and pulled the boat down to Redding, California for my brother to sell. I took a licking on both. We were rather pleased and happy to be going to Panama. A soldier is sorta like a cow, to a cow the grass is greener on the other side of the fence; to a soldier, the place he has just left, or the place he is going is the best.

CHAPTER FIFTEEN
More of the Good Years and Army Career Ends

We drove across country and flew out of Charleston, South Carolina for the Canal Zone, November fifty-nine. We landed at Albrook AFB and had to travel across the Isthmus to where I was to be stationed at Ft. Gulick, I was assigned quarters at Fort Davis, a few miles from Gulick. Cathy was very concerned about where we were to live, having just left the only home she knew in Washington. There are many shacks and huts in Panama. I saw a terrible looking shack, and said to Cathy, "Look Cathy, there's our new house." Tears came into her eyes, she was so pitiful that I didn't tease her anymore about Panama's houses and where we were to live. I was assigned as an automotive maintenance instructor, to The School of The Americas. The School taught trades and Military subjects to the Military from South and Central America. During the month of December and first two weeks of January I had to do all my instructor training.

Such things as learning how to operate projection equipment, CBR training course and review lesson plans. The new class started in January so we were very busy preparing for the incoming class. Our duty uniform for the instructors during this phase was fatigues. The first day I went to work after weeks of instructors school in early January, the Colonel came to the break room and said, "Sgt. Spivey, you are out of uniform."

I was shocked, thinking my uniform was fine, for I am never out of uniform. I snapped to attention and asked, "Why is that, Sir?"

He answered, "I have appointed you to be the Senior Instructor for the Department effective today, so the uniform for you is Class A."

I was surprised and very pleased. I stayed in this job until I transferred to U.S. Army Caribbean Headquarters in the Summer sixty-two.

Shortly after we arrived in Panama, Debbie had a very high fever that lasted for a few days. We were very worried and concerned, the doctors did not know the cause for the fever. A short while later Debbie began having problems breathing, doctors couldn't find the cause for that either. They suggested or recommended that we try air conditioning. There was no AC in Military quarters, and very little anywhere in the Canal Zone. Besides on an enlisted pay scale, expensive. We purchased two window units for our quarters, and that more or less solved her breathing problems, we were very thankful. With temperatures hardly ever below eighty-five or so it helped all of us tremendously. Particular at nights without AC it was impossible to enjoy a good night rest.

For several weeks we lived at Fort Davis, then we moved to Fort Gulick, both on the Caribbean (Atlantic) side of the Canal Zone. Fort Gulick is where The School of The Americas was located, (The School is located at

Fort Benning now, ninety-three). Also, the PX, Commissary, Theater, and recreation facilities. It was just two short blocks to the office where I worked. There was much spit and polish required in my work. There were many VIPS (Very Important People) visitors to the School and our Department. I assisted in conducting these informative tours. The weather, the humidity, and sweat made it necessary to change uniforms for each tour. In just a short while and particular if one sat, one's uniform looked as if it had been slept in. At times I stood around up to an hour or so waiting for the tour to arrive. Each week I gave four to six hours of instruction, (classroom). I liked the School and the people I worked with. The Department Chief was one of best Officers that I ever had the pleasure to work for or with. Colonel Daubert, the Department Chief, and Colonel Belisle (Appendix One), two of the best that I have ever served with. Compared to other Posts there was not much stress at the School, such as grabass, training, inspections and such, if one performed, no problems. In Panama, there are two seasons, wet and hot, and dry and hot. We were all contented while in the Canal Zone. We all stayed busy with traveling around a bit, picnics, fishing, and me, golfing a bit. I never was any good at it. I attended a few off duty classes taking English, History, Spanish, and Accounting; these courses convinced me that I was not an apt student. We participated in church, and the scouts. Plus, I had to do a certain amount of physical training so I could pass the PT test. Beta was a good walker. She could stay with me on my four mile walks, that was twice a week or so, took us forty-five minutes or a little less, her legs being shorter, she had to jog a little.

I was promoted to Master Sergeant E8 while I was Senior Instructor, A&A Department at The School of The Americas. The Colonel or Department Chief was transferred to USARCARIB Headquarters and shortly afterward, a Sergeant Major E9 vacancy occurred. The Colonel told me if I would transfer over there, he would promote me. It took some doing, but I eventually got the transfer. Two times, I applied for transfer and two times it was disapproved. The third time I asked to see the Commandant to plead my case. I was told I could see the Commandant, but it wouldn't do any good, I went to the Commandant's office and before I said anything, he starting blowing much as to what a good man I was and what a good job I was doing. Also saying, that he couldn't afford to loose me by letting me transfer out of the school. When he had finished talking, I had a few words that went like this. "I have tried to do the best job that I could do at this school. I think I've done a good job. And because I have done a good job, I am being penalized. For if I am allowed to transfer to Headquarters USARCARIB, I will be assigned to an E9 position. Just in the past few weeks a MSgt., a good instructor messed up a bit, he was transferred from the School in two days. Here I have tried to be an excellent instructor, for that, I will not be allowed to transfer and be promoted to Sergeant Major. I would like very much to be given this opportunity." After what I said, the Commandant very reluctantly approved the transfer. I was grateful. I was promoted to SMaj. six weeks later. Three days after being promoted I demoted. There were some complaints that I did not meet the requirements of time in the Army, time in grade, and had less time in grade (E-8) than a few others that were in E-9 positions. Further, that waivers were required before I could be promoted. By the time the next quote came, I had the necessary waivers to be promoted, and I made E9 the next month.

We moved to the Pacific side and lived at Ft. Clayton until June Sixty-four. Our activities didn't change. The duty in the Canal Zone was slow compared to other places I had been and we would have stayed longer than four and a half years if we could have. We were not permitted to extend our tour in Panama. The fishing in Panama was better than any place I had ever been. A few families that we chummed around with, including us made a couple of barges with fifty five-gallon drums, plus I had a small boat that we had a lot of fun speeding over the lake. One could depend on the fishing to be good. Fishing and cooking out on Madden Lake was our favorite place. We caught Brazilian bream that averaged a pound and a quarter. Salt water fishing on the Pacific side was good, we had many different types of fish to fish for. To top it all, shrimp were plentiful and cheap, twenty-five cents per pound. For some I suppose the greatest draw back was keeping busy and staying out of trouble. One problem is that they didn't adapt to the slow life style, and get involved in hobbies instead of partying and boozing.

For several weeks we lived at Fort Davis, then we moved to Fort Gulick, both on the Caribbean (Atlantic) side of the Canal Zone. Fort Gulick is where The School of The Americas was located, (The School is located at Fort Benning now, ninety-three). Also, the PX, Commissary, Theater, and recreation facilities. It was just two short blocks to the office where I worked. There was much spit and polish required in my work. There were many VIPS (Very Important People) visitors to the School and our Department. I assisted in conducting these informative tours. The weather, the humidity, and sweat made it necessary to change uniforms for each tour. In just a short while and particular if one sat, one's uniform looked as if it had been slept in. At times I stood around up to an hour or so waiting for the tour to arrive. Each week I gave four to six hours of instruction, (classroom). I liked the School and the people I worked with. The Department Chief was one of best Officers that I ever had the pleasure to work for or with. Colonel Daubert, the Department Chief, and Colonel Belisle (Appendix One), two of the best that I have ever served with. Compared to other Posts there was not much stress at the School, such as grabass, training, inspections and such, if one performed, no problems.

We moved to Fort Clayton on the Pacific side into practically new ranch style quarters, still no air conditioning in Army quarters. We were spoiled, being accustomed to AC since arriving in Panama, we did not want to forgo the comfort AC, therefore, I installed two window units. So that our habit of moving a lot would not be tarnished, we lived in four different sets of quarters in four and a half years while in Panama. Having a transit (moving a couple times yearly, it seemed like) type of career, that I suppose that over the years that the numerous moves we have made is sorta a record. The job was different at USAR-CARIB, a dab more stress. Still a good assignment without many pucker factors. It was not very many people that were dumb enough to try to give the Sergeant Major a hard time anyway. Most everyone liked duty in the Canal Zone, if it was just a dab cooler they couldn't be run out. When the time to make assignment choices in the States came, we selected Post Ordnance, Fort Lewis, Washington, Fort McPherson, Georgia, and Alaska. When I received orders for the Fourth Infantry Division, I was very disappointed. I pushed the panic button. I certainly didn't want to go back to the Fourth Division, Post Ordnance, Fort Lewis, but not the Fourth Division. I solicited help from my Chief, and I starting trying a dab of string pulling too. I made connection and got the orders changed to Headquarters Third Army, Fort McPherson. About the same time the colonel was successful in getting me assigned to Post Ordnance Fort Lewis. A hard choice for me, my choice was, Fort McPherson. I was sorta embarrassed by not taking the assignment the Colonel got for me. We scheduled our leaving Panama to arrive in Charleston South Carolina about the same time Jimmy would get out of school. He was attending Carlisle at Bamberg South Carolina. The flight out of Panama was a bit stressful. At the most westward point going around Cuba lightning struck the plane. U.S. chartered planes did not fly over Cuba then. The radio antennas were broken, the antennas slapping and scratching the fuselage, making an awful noise, the main radios were knocked out, one engine went kaput, and it was a bit scary. The pilot told us that everything was under control, nothing to worry about, for the Coast Guard was sending out a plane to escort us to Miami. Most were calm and naive, but my question was, If everything was all right, why was the plane coming to meet us. I suppose it was alright for we did arrive in Miami in fine shape many hours late. It took five hours to repair the plane and we were eight hours late getting into Charleston.

Our friends, Willie, and Inez Ziegler, that lived at Walterboro, close to Charleston met us with Jimmy. He would stay with them at times when he would be out of school for a day or two. We needed an automobile, so I started looking. We did not locate what we wanted. Kicking tires is an exhausting hot job in South Carolina in June. We went into the show room to cool off, in the show room sat a new Mercury Comet, that cost about twenty-three hundred. I was tired of looking at cars, so just for conversation I told the salesman I would give him two thousand for it, bottom line. He said he would have to check on that. I wasn't expecting to be taken seriously on the offer. They did and I bought it. We were the proud owners of a 1964 Comet four door and wanted to get on with our leave visiting kinfolks. The girls were in a rush to see their Puppy, that was in Columbus Georgia at my brothers. We had sent the Puppy to the States a few days before we left. We had much catching up to do, visiting some of the folks we had not seen in a few years. In our family we do believe in keeping in touch. After ten days I went to Fort McPherson, in Atlanta to look for a house for us. Atlanta had plenty of houses available, the trouble was to find a house we liked in the right place. I did not want to spend hours on the road every day. After compiling a list I returned to Andalusia and then back to Atlanta for Beta to pick the house. It was not an easy task, our likes did not go together at times. We finally settled on a new house in SW Atlanta off Campbellton Road. We did not have any furniture at all. Looking for furniture and making comparisons is a hassle and much aggravation. After looking all over Metro Atlanta we finely got the house furnished after many months. No great setbacks nor burdensome problems while at Fort McPherson. We were a happy family living the abundant life. My Army career of almost twenty-two years ended 1 June nineteen-sixty-five, I have no regrets, for almost twenty-two years the Army was my life.

RETROSPECT:
The Second Twenty, or Forty

Retrospect The First Twenty was very easy, I knew what I wanted to say. That is not the way this is going, the Second Twenty is much different; So, I will close with the last four decades or so. The changes in all aspects of life were phenomenal. Even though with all these many changes, somehow the changes in life style seemed to be gradual. This is rather odd, for in the past four decades there have been more changes than any time in history. We, the family, went from a root hog, or die poor, to a tranquil, pleasing abundant life. During this time I learned to enjoy much that in the thirties and forties I knew nothing about, or even dreamed of, or existed.

I am blessed with a caring, loving wife, and children. There is no way that I can measure these blessings. I enjoy my family, my friends, my country, my Church, and I love them all dearly; and now we are blessed with four grandchildren, they are the top priority now. My concerns are much different from what they were in the decades past. I have much concern for my grandchildren and family. This is the reason that I have so much concern about my country; somewhat of a quote, what is good for my country is good for them, the family. I would like for many things to be better, without so much apathy, and a Government that is for the People.

Our Government, and some of the people are now attempting and doing so much that is contrary to nature, to God, common sense and common decency. This causes me much concern for my Grandchildren.

I will close with this plea, Be concerned for your country; be active, tell it the way it is; and search for a way to make your Country better for you and your family. GOD BLESS.

As I See It, and From the Heart

This will be a mixture of many things of life and some might be controversial, but it is I. In this retrospect I hope to show contrast in virtuous living and the abundant life obtained from it. And the innermost thoughts of a Patriot that loves God, his Country and Family. It is not written with the intent to offend anyone. If I were asked to describe a typical American I could not do it. And if I did no one would agree with me. But I would like to make an attempt by making comparisons of people that have some characterizations of what a good American might have or be, and of some that do not have a measurable amount of good character. This does not mean that we are all good or all bad. Nor does it mean that we are to love one group and hate the other.

Would I rather be more like, or for my family to be more like, the following?

Tom Landry	or	Red Fox
Roger Staubach	or	Magic Johnson
Jack Kemp	or	Woope Goldberg
Lucille Ball	or	Jane Fonda
Debbie Reynolds	or	' Roseanne Barr
Colin Powell	or	Phil Donahue
Jimmy Carter	or	Ramsey Clark
San Nunn	or	Ted Kennedy
Jean Kilpatrick	or	Donna Shalala
Sandra Day O'Conner	or	Joycelyn Elders

One could go on, and on. Realizing there is good and bad in all, it is still an easy choice for me. To me, people that made and make America what it is, are people that have in some degree, HONOR, COMMON DECENCY, CHARACTER, HERITAGE, and WILLINGNESS TO SERVE.

Now one other comparison is, do any of us remember who were Cabinet Members in the various Cabinets of, Presidents Kennedy, Nixon, Carter, Reagan, Bush, and now Clinton's. Need I say more?! The difference in character, dignity, respect, prestige, honor, and common decency, is STRIKING!

What is a family? My Grandparents were married at a young age, these marriages lasted a lifetime. They were Christians, active Church Members, and God fearing. They taught their children, my twenty Uncles and Aunts, right from wrong. None were divorced, no drug addicts, nor perverts. My cousins, my generation, off hand I don't know the exact number, but approximately seventy-six. I don't know all of them, of these that I know and/or have heard about, there have been a few divorces, but no derelicts or whatever, nor perverts. All around I see families that do not have any family relationship; don't know where their family members are, and don't seem to care. Is this the character and traditions we knew many years ago? Is this, common decency?

There is no way that many of our supposed dignified elite can be respected, or can honestly be accepted as role models. These politicians, professional sports jocks, super elite entertainers, some TV preachers, shysters, that we have in our society today, and with a gang of them in Washington, D.C. now. Fifty or so years ago, they, repeat they, would have been considered the scum of society. This is a fact, not rhetoric.

History proves that when a family, a tribe, or a country leaves their sense of common decency and virtuous heritage and traditions, they self destruct. In our day history will prove that, any person, family, country, that turns to anti life, anti-God, perversion, the crazy teachings to our youth, will self destruct.

Our most honored, respected dignified men of our Country, all had a sense of common decency, virtuous traditions, heritage, this is fact, not hot air. What does history tell us about George Washington, he was truthful, he was also first in the hearts of the people; Abraham

Lincoln, honest Abe; Nathan Hale, regretted that he had only one life to give for his Country; he served, and he gave his life; Pershing, MacAurthur, these are some that served above and beyond the call of duty. They all knew and had common decency, heritage, traditions. What can we say about the gang in Washington D.C. now, nineteen ninety-three? The liars, anti life, anti God, draft dodgers, perverts, ultra liberal, and odd ball socialists flower people from the sixties.

Quite a contrast, huh?

The traditions of my Grandparents, Uncles, and Aunts are most of the contributing factors of what I am, or what I am not. Most lived three score and ten or more without Medicare, none were on welfare, they lived the abundant life by working for it, and putting much value on their traditions, none were wealthy or materialistic well off.

I must add this due to the unpleasant condition of our Government. I am very concerned about the many people in high places of responsibility in our government; people THAT DO NOT HAVE, CHARACTER, COMMON DECENCY, as most of our forefathers had.

The only thing or things that separate the human species, (man), from other species of life, is, the virtues of common decency, fortitude, diligence, heritage, dignity, fidelity, all the rest and, duty, honor, for their family and country. Without these traits of common decency man would be animals, like monkeys in the forest, or dogs of the streets. On the other hand, repeat, families, tribes, societies that leave their common decencies and become liars, anti God (religion), militant perverts, ultra-liberal odd ball socialists, and derelict flower people of sixties, will self destruct.

A Doughboys Narrative •

I ask you to make comparisons of people in Government of the past and present. Any difference? THINK, who, can support these socialistic flower people of the sixties?

THE FINALE

A Doughboys Narrative •

APPENDIX ONE

M urice A. Belisle, Colonel, U.S. Army Retired entered the Army at Fort Devens, Massachusetts Summer 1941. Colonel Belisle was the most rememberable and outstanding Officer that I had the pleasure to serve under. The Colonel was my Platoon leader, Executive Officer, and Commanding Officer. As an enlisted man serving in his unit for many years, I am certain he's a dedicated American, a soldier who served his country above and beyond the call of duty. The Colonel is an Officer that one will always remember and admire. (Spivey)

BY
Colonel Murice A. Belisle

These are very informal notes made with only minor research:

My first command was with the 4th Platoon, "E" Company, 26th Infantry. What a group! Sergeant Hardy and a rough assortment of anything but new recruits; it took me some time to get so I felt at ease. I recall one incident at

Fort Devens when I walked into the barracks and everything was in disorder. Sergeant Murphy was drunk and the platoon was not at attention. I went into Murphy's room and we had it out. I challenged him, we pushed each other around a bit, but did not fight. I gave him one hour to get the platoon in order or I would end his career. He promised to get all in order. When I returned, the place looked more like an Army barracks.

We landed on the beach at Les Andalouses, west of Oran, Algeria, (North Africa). With no opposition on the beach, we dropped part of our ammunition in an orange grove. (We had taken three days ammo and rations ashore). That was all that was immediately available for the invasion. There was no action until after day light. (We had landed at midnight, "E" Company was separated at the beach area). Captain Mara and half of the Company joined us later.

The enemy's first reaction was with artillery as we neared Cape Falcon, which overlooked and protected Mers El Kebir, (the major North African port of the French Navy). This is where the British Navy destroyed much of the French Navy. The French truly hated the British for this disaster and that is why we wore the U.S. flag on our helmets.

The next day we, the 2nd Battalion, captured the fort at Cape Falcon. And the next day, D+3, it was all over.

The next action took place in Tunisia, but on the trip there we camped at a place near Constantine (I think) and near an air strip for B-25's. Some of our great machine gunners hitched rides on bombing missions as gunners.. I later found out.

Our first attack took place in the Qusseltia Valley. Actually, the artillery and mortars really cleared the mountain which was our objective. There were only a few dead and injured Italian soldiers there when we arrived. We were counter attacked after several days. Captain Mara was transferred to "H" Company, because several officers were captured at the time of the counterattack and I took over "E" Company at that time.

Our next action came about fifteen days after our arrival at Quesseltia (Kairouan). I was called to the Battalion Headquarters and General Roosevelt advised us of the breakthrough at Kasserine Pass. "E" Company was to take the highest peak in the area (Djbel Barb Rou). The Regiment was to go to Kasserine in relief. As you recall, there were no roads to our target.

We took off cross-country practically by compass. The weather was horrible.. (typical First Division weather).. the ground was muddy.. the mountains steep. At one point we met a French Officer on horseback and asked directions. It was most tedious, especially for our weapons platoon with the heavy loads. Once we reached Barb Rou, there was no resistance and little to see except for a nomadic tribe. By this time, we were out of rations and I purchased a lamb from a tribesman which Al Collins butchered and all of us had a bite of chewy meat. Elements of the First Division Reconnaissance came to relieve us a few days later.

The landing on Sicily was started at midnight; I recall the ride into the beach as the counter fire by our Navy put out the search lights and guns. The most dangerous time occurred on the first day when the enemy tanks got almost to the beach. Our artillery was firing point blank at them until they finally retreated. That same night the Airborne guys were making a "practice" jump into the beachhead and our Navy plastered them. The Germans were making an air raid at the same time.

I left the Company at the end of the Sicilian Campaign. Captain Jesse Jarvis took over. One morning shortly after arriving at our camp site, I believe it was Al Collins, came to my tent and told me that "E" Company was about to revolt. It appears that Jarvis, just in from a Replacement

Depot, was treating the Company as recruits. As I recall, after a march, he insisted on having a foot inspection. I went to see him, but he was hard nosed and said he was right. I went to Colonel Daniel and recommended that this guy go to an administrative job. And then, you guys got one of the best, Lieutenant Ozel Smoot, as your Commanding Officer.

APPENDIX TWO

Vaughn E. Manning, CWO4 U.S. Army Retired writes his personal feelings of joining a combat unit December nineteen forty-four. I met First Sergeant Manning when I rejoined Company E 26th Infantry early January nineteen forty-five after a lengthy stay in the hospital (August through December 1944). We became very good friends and Comrades. Many years later, I saw Manning's name in the Society of First Division paper, THE BRIDGEHEAD SENTINEL. I immediately called him and it has been a wonderful and joyful experience reestablishing our friendship. Manning had a long distinguished Army career, enlisted 1937 as a private and retired in sixty-three as a Chief Warrant Office W4. He was awarded the CIB, BS w/V, and Oak Leaf Cluster, ACM w/Oak Leaf Clusters and many Letters of Appreciation and Efficiency while serving his Country. I honor and respect men such as Mr. Manning. (Spivey)

My Feelings Upon My First Entry Into Combat
By Vaughn E. Manning

I will try to explain my feelings upon first entry into combat. I joined an Infantry Rifle company, Co. E 26th Infantry Regiment First Infantry Division. At the beginning of the Battle of the Bulge at Butgenbach, Belgium on 21 December 1944. It was snowing and visibility was approximately twenty-five yards, and the snow between one and two feet deep. German tanks were roaming around looking for American soldiers, who were located in foxholes and demolished buildings. I had walked approximately two miles after being dropped off of a truck and was instructed where to go. I finally found the command post located in a half basement at the end of a demolished stone dairy barn. I crawled down into a small room containing four men.

As my eyes became accustomed to the darkness, I saw a 1st Lieutenant talking on a radio to the platoon sergeants. I soon found out that he was the Company Commander. He saw the stripes on my arm and asked, if I was his new First Sergeant. I told him that I was. He then told me that he would talk to me later. I should point out that I was actually an artillery first sergeant and had been converted to Infantry. I had three years' infantry training prior to entering Artillery, but many things had changed.

The Company Commander was giving orders to the platoons on how to handle the situation as they were being attacked; and I had a few moments to try and collect my thoughts and adapt myself to the battle that was going on around me. It was impossible for me to grasp the situation or visualize what was going on outside of that bunker. Everyone knows that in any situation the lack of knowledge causes fear. This fear and frustration made me feel completely helpless. The feeling began to subside only after the attack was repulsed and I began to help the wounded and found out the general location of the platoons.

I think if I had entered combat with the unit my feelings would have been somewhat different. I think everyone entering combat for the first time has a feeling of loneliness and wanting so much to speak to someone but just do not know what to say.

A Brave Young Soldier's Entry Into a Combat Unit
By Vaughn E. Manning

I would like to relate a true story about a young soldier reporting to my company for his first combat duty. The Company was in a small village and had a severe fire fight in which there were three dead and several were wounded. We placed the dead in a room of the house where the Company's CP was located. Several recruits reported in as a group and one asked if we had any Chicago gangsters in the unit. I had a small candle burning and could see that he was a very young boy. I asked him why he wanted the information and asked him his age. He said that he was also a Chicago gangster and was seventeen years old. I had a small pinpoint flashlight and asked him to come with me as there were three in the next room. I shined the light on the dead soldiers. He opened his mouth but did not make a sound. I then assigned him to a platoon and instructed him to listen very closely to all his instructions and to forget about how tough he was. He was never mentioned for a decoration or an award for bravery. (The point of this story is, if a replacement did not listen, learn and adapt very quickly, his chances of survival any length time were slim to nil. Without knowledge of the art of survival his time was measured in hours or days). (SPIVEY)

A Doughboys Narrative ●

APPENDIX THREE

Sergeant Clyde E. DeWitte served in Company E 26th Infantry Regiment from November 1940 through March 1945. He served with distinction as a gunner, squad leader, and section sergeant. Sergeant DeWitte was awarded the Combat Infantryman's Badge, Bronze Star w/V, for valor, w/Oak Leaf Cluster, Purple Heart, eight Campaign Stars, and Arrowhead for three invasions. Clyde gave his best, was greatly respected and honored by his fellow Soldiers. As a friend, team mate, and Comrade in Arms, we served in the same platoon for almost five years. I have much respect for Clyde and hold him in the highest esteem. There is just no way that I can explain the degree of feelings between us as Comrades in Arms. (Spivey)

What I Saw and Felt, WWII
By Sergeant Clyde E. DeWitte

My Army life/career started fifteen November 1940 at Fort Devens, Massachusetts. For the first three weeks of my Army career, I was on kitchen police duty. About the same time the Army started getting in the inductees that were given a deal that allowed potential draftees to volunteer for one year instead of being drafted for an indefinite period was offered. (That deal like so many government deals was a sucker deal. Those that took the deal like the rest of us, didn't get out until after the War). Anyway, I was in the right place at the right time, for in just a few days I was an EXPERT at washing pots, pans, and dishes or whatever and an overnight EXPERT at peeling spuds. The Army cooks were famous for messing up everything and bossing the KP help.

Fort Devens was a choice assignment for me and I liked it there very much. We were billeted in new, modern brick barracks with stainless steel kitchen equipment, electric potato peelers, electric dish washing machines and such. It was like being in college. I remember that one soldier was too tall for the bunks and was discharged. It was a good life for a while then the hard work began, training day and night, over and over, with no end in sight. We spent a few weeks at Cape Cod, (Buzzards Bay) for amphibious training. This was something new for everyone. Getting off the ship the hard way, going down a cargo net into a small landing craft that was bobbing and bouncing around like a cork. Then after getting wet and sand all over you, from the run across the beach we would return and then climb up the net back onto the ship. That eventually got tiring and very boring. I think the ship was the U.S.S. Kent, an old rust bucket. Following this was the amphibious training at or close to New River, North Carolina on the U.S.S. Leonard Wood. This was for a couple of months with a week or ten days at Charleston, South Carolina. FUN TIME! One of the ships boilers had to be repaired and then back to training and the beaches. These were busy times for us and before we could get things shaped up we were off again. This time to the big, big maneuvers in and around Fort Bragg, North Carolina. In early December we returned to Fort Devens and then it was the start of World War II for us.

January/February 1942, more amphibious training landing at Virginia Beach, Virginia where we almost froze. There was snow on the beach, it was cold and we were wet. Should I say more? Very shortly after returning to Fort Devens once again we were on our way to Camp Blanding, Florida. As I recall, there was plenty of sand and dust. At Blanding, I participated in a big parade, The First and the 36th Infantry Divisions parading, honoring General Sir John Dill, British Army General Staff. We paraded with full field gear, and me, carrying a 60MM mortar. Marching with a 60MM mortar in a parade is a bit awkward. At Blanding, we were pushed almost beyond the limits of our durability, running, forced marches, obstacle courses, and you name it, we did it. Sometimes I think they (the Brass) wanted to see just how miserable they could make it. Then there was the misery of the joint infantry, tank, and direct air support exercises at Fort Benning, Georgia. The May/June heat, dust and sand, hills, and running after the tanks almost finished us off. this was for only one reason, making us tough for combat, so they said, and maybe it paid off.

The big day came when we went to Indiantown Gap, Pennsylvania. There we started preparing to ship out for overseas and the War. Sunday, two August nineteen forty-two, we waved goodbye to the Statue of Liberty and our great Country, not knowing, when we would be back, where we were going, and sometimes why. We were on HMS Queen Mary for a voyage to Gourock, Scotland. This was another new experience for most of us and with nothing better to do, we counted flying fish and porpoises swimming along the side of the bow. Scotland was the only place that I ever saw that had swamps on the sides of the hills. After a short stay for us at Tidworth Barracks near Salisbury, England, we were on the move again.

Getting our equipment, some new weapons and then back to Scotland for more amphibious training on HMS Warwick Castle. Practice, practice over and over, we did not know for what? Or where, but there was always rumors on top of rumors.

October 1942 we boarded HMS Monarch of Bermuda and when at sea we received the news that North Africa was our destination. We would make an assault landing at Les Andalouses, which was a dozen or so miles west of Oran, Algeria. This operation was more or less a mixture of foul-ups with good luck or something, it ended well. This was sort of a prelude to our ordeal with Hitler's army.

Tunisia: I was on an outpost on one of the many hills that we never ran out of and it rained all the time I was there. There were also some Singhalese soldiers with me. They had the reputation of being very brutal, cruel, bloody fighters. In a fight they would bite or cut their opponents ear off, it would not bother them one bit and they were given a bonus for the ears they collected. In the foothills at about the center of the front was the town of Constantine, a hill town, congenial and peaceful, no war was going on there.

Things got tougher as we took hill after hill, (209, 409, 545 they became meaningless) El Geuttar, Mateur...they said, we were going home after we captured Tunisia. Of course, it was a rumor, but what a cruel one.

After Tunisia, we got ready for Sicily. This meant more training, amphibious exercises, conditioning. Plus, the never ending training was, next to combat, the thing we hated most. Our losses in Tunisia and Sicily were substantial. Late summer we got a new team to lead us, General Terry Allen and General Teddy Roosevelt were re-assigned elsewhere. They had a good rapport with the troops and just about everyone liked them.

October forty-three we left Sicily for England to re-group and build up our division again. Also, we continued with the never ending training. About all I can say about D-Day at Normandy is that it was hell. Those of us that made it were very fortunate. God bless the ones who didn't. I was wounded in France and was in a hospital there, I don't remember where. I had to have shots every four hours and the nurse would wake me, and say, "roll over." One day she came in and said, "roll over," but I couldn't. While I was sleeping some of the patients had sewed my sheets together so that I could not roll over. Needless to say, I was very concerned, I had head wounds and it unsettled me until the nurse found the problem. It was a terrible joke to me.

Discharged from the hospital I went back to Company E and on into Belgium. There was one family that I met that knew of my Father and invited some of us to dinner. My father's family was originally from Belgium. The family brought out all the goodies they had been hiding. What a feast! Quite different from C rations.

We moved on into Aachen, Germany. It was one of the fiercest battles we had fought. One time we were in a cellar and outside on the street was a German tank that we could see through the window. We had only carbines, pistols and mortars, we were helpless. You cannot knock out a Tiger tank with a carbine. The Germans finally moved out and we moved on up the street going house to house searching for and pushing out the Germans. Going by one of the building I heard someone calling for help and checked it out. What a surprise when I saw who it was. It was my buddy that I had hung around with. I patched him up and got the medics who started him on his way back to the hospital. The Germans were desperately trying to hold Aachen. They threw everything at us, buzz bombs, screaming meemies, and just about anything that was available. I really don't know how any of us made it through alive and in our mind.

By now we were wondering when all this would end and what our fate would be. We knew that we were fugitives from the law of averages. Finally I got word the night before we were to cross the Rhine River that I was going home. We went back to France, got on a Liberty Ship with a lot of prisoners and headed for the USA.

I can never say enough about serving with the finest men and Soldiers any one would ever want to serve with.

APPENDIX FOUR

Manning'S Notebook

Vaughn Manning was 1st Sgt. Dec. 1944 till the end of WWII. He kept a small notebook to aid him in making out the daily report, (Morning Report) not even combat stopped these daily reports. These notes are form 8 Mar. through 30 April, there are 32 daily entries during these 53 days. Some were made while walking, some while using a small penlight, most were made under combat conditions. The weather in the Rhine/Roer Valleys was a mixture of misty rain, snow, with slush and mud, at times miserably cold. By the middle of March the weather began to improve, becoming bearable to nice.

We can see by these notes that combat is a mixed bag, with lulls in the fighting. After some of the fierce battles the Doughboys are physically, mentally, exhausted, and a day or to rejuvenate was welcomed. Units would leap frog over the company and would have a day or two off the line. At times there was a vicious, bloody, desperate, and seemingly a never ending struggle all around. Days seemed like weeks, weeks like months. This life or death struggle, misery from the elements, the agony of combat, is undescribable.

As we read these few notes let our imagination take us to Roer and Rhine Valleys, March/April 1945. The push to end the War in Europe started in February. We are making steady progress, intense fighting taking towns and villages daily. Our causalities were moderate to heavy averaging more than five daily. I will include only a few entrees. These notes are copied from the notebook as written, no corrections are made.

53 Days - 8 March - 30 April, 1945

32 Daily Entries, 63 WIA, 3 KIA, 3 MIA, 12 SICK, 1 SIW, 2 ACCID, 2 AWOL, plus 14 KIA at Orshed, PLUS 42 WIA or KIA at Liblar. (Total, approx. 142).

15 Mar Company left Bonn riding at 0830, detrucking at Unkelbach Ger. 1030 left walking across the Rhine River to Rhinebertback Ger. and then down to Ohlenberg. Distance overall 25 miles. 1 AWOL, 1 sick, 1 SIW.

18 Mar Company left Henberg 0230 walking. Attacked Oshied 0530 taking 20 prisoners in open field. Co. G. had completely taken town when we entered at 0530. The enemy offered little resistance. 2nd Platoon pushed out to Reischett and secured objective at 0930. Company left this position at 2000 attacking. Objective taken at 2300. Prisoners taken from both objectives. (These 20 prisoners taken by the company were flushed out of farm building that the 4th platoon entered and by mistake. The new platoon leader took the wrong road. Another snafu. Spivey). 1 MIA, 9 WIA, 1 accident, 1 sick.

19 Mar Company in same position until 2000. Left walking to the N.E., Objective German Airport. Company meeting slight enemy resistance and began receiving

artillery and mortar fire at 2400. Still moving forward meeting stiff resistance of mortar and N.G. fire. WIA 17

20 Mar Company continued moving forward meeting stiff resistance. Took off (objective) 0400, 8 replacements

21 Mar Company left this position at 2100 walking and took over position held by Co. G 18th Infantry at Eudenbach, Germany. Enemy activity very heavy with rocket, mortar and artillery fire before leaving for new positions. 1 WIA, 2 sick, Left Eudenbach at 2400

22 Mar Company in same position. Enemy activity slight with scattered artillery, mortar and sniper fire. Company received mail.

23 Mar Left Eudenbach at 0030 reaching Boseroth at 0130. Men were served hot lunch and were billeted in houses. Left Boseroth at 0800 at __0900. Billeted in houses, received 8 replacements.

25 Mar Left 0800 riding trucks. Detrucking at Cord 698-342 and loaded on tanks and rode to Lindshiel, left walking at 2400 attacking Marlheip. Meeting very slight resistance and secured objective at 0100. Cover _____Captured 20 prisoners, one tank, 2 SP Guns, knocking 4 mortars in position. 6 WIA

26 Mar Men spent day resting and cleaning up. Left Lindecheid at 1900 walking. Attacked Eitorf 2400 meeting very slight enemy resistance. 1 shot accident, 1 sick

2 April Left 0700 riding. Arriving in Meiste 1800. No enemy activity. Set up surrounding defensive positions. Distance traveled 110 miles.

3 April Company left Meiste walking at 0900. Arrived at Hemmeron, Ger. 1000 taking surrounding defensive

positions. Distance 2 miles. 3 hot meals served, 6 returned from hospital.

6 April Company left Hemmeron at 1730 riding. Arrived at objective at 1900 relieving 1st Recon Group. Took no enemy activity. Pick up 7 enemy stragglers as prisoners. Company received hot meals.

12 April Left Kalefeld 0030 riding at Nienstedt at 0500, left Nienstedt _____arrived 1430, arrived in Oberhiette at 1600. Going into position enemy activity slight, took two prisoners.

14 April Company left position at 1400 walking on the attack. Enemy activity strong. Company moving forward clearing enemy and road blocks. Inflicting many casualties and taking 6 prisoners. 2 WIA

15 April Company moving forward meeting stiff resistance and took our objective Tarhaus, Germany at 0930. Set up all around defence. Contracting friendly units on our left. Company took 120 prisoners, Tarfhaid knocking out 1 SP

17-18 April Company attacked 0830 moving forward meeting stiff resistance. Move on objective and secure at 1330 taking 50 combat prisoners and series of hospitals with estimate 1000 patients and medical aid persons. 3 KIA, 6 WIA, 1 sick

22 April Company in same defense. No enemy activity. Company took 7 prisoners. Men attended church and movies. 4 men given medals

23 April 4 came in (from hosp) 26 April 9 came in (from hosp)

ROSTERS
Company E 26th Infantry
February/March

Rosters of Company E of December 1941, five officers, two hundred and one enlisted men. On the 1945 roster were, five officers, with one lined out. Enlisted were one hundred and eightyeight, with fifty-four lined out. Present for duty were four officers, and one hundred and thirty-four enlisted men. The purpose for these rosters is just to give us some idea of the rapid changes in personnel in an infantry rifle company of the First Division. There are only four men that are on both rosters, these four had been wounded one to three times, had been hospitalized and returned to Company E. The same applies to D-Day, there were four left of the over two hundred that landed at Omaha Beach, 6 June 1944.

COMPANY "E" 26th INFANTRY
FIRST INFANTRY DIVISION
FORT DEVENS, MASSACHUSETTS
DECEMBER 1941

COMPANY COMMANDER
1st LT. JOHN N. DAVIS

FIRST LIEUTENANTS
JOHN D. HANDLON   ANTHONY M. SARRETT

SECOND LIEUTENANTS
MAURICE A. BELISLE   CHARLES P. OLIVER   AZEL J. TAGGART

FIRST SERGEANT
ISRAEL SEDOFSKY

STAFF SERGEANTS
ARTHUR BRYANT

SERGEANTS

MERRILL V. ARNOLD	JOHN F. BAARS	ROBERT BERGERON
CLARNCE CRIM	ALFRED G. COLLINS	WALTER J. DONOHUE
JURENE B. EVERSEN	KARL D. FARLEY	PAUL GOLDSTEIN
MAURICE GRIFFIN	JAMES A HARTY	WILFRED R. HAUSLER
DENNIS A. LEGERE	CHARLES W. MERRILL	JAMES C. MURGHY

JAMES E. OVERTURF   ROLAND J. PHILLIPS   FRANK RIZZUTO
JOHN J. ROGERS   HENRY SMITH   EMANUEL G. STRANGE

CORPORALS

FRANCESCO ANTOCICCO	ORVILLE L. ARMSTRONG	GROVER C. BAILY
ELDIE A. BLEZINGER	THURLOW J. CUNLIFFE	JOHN DAKIN
PAUL T. FEENEY	FRANK T. GABRYELSKI	JOE F. HUTCHISON
ROBERT L. LUND	FRANCIS J. MILLMORE	NEWTON O. PESCHEL
JAMES T. REYNOLDS	ROBERT SIMONE	SAMUEL D. SPIVEY
ANTHONY J. WALCZAK	NOEL D. MOCK	

PRIVATES FIRST CLASS

DAVID L. BAIRD	JOSEPH BOLDIGA	JOSE V. BRASIL
MAURICE R. CARTIER	JOSEPH R. COSTIGAN	FERNAND A. COTE
NORMAN O. DAGENAIS	SYDNEY S. DAMB	HENRY J. DOXEY
MAYNARD B. ELLIS	THOMAS R. ENGLISH	JOSE L. A. ENO
EARL E. COCKER	FRANK J. FARRELL	LEOPOLD FILA
JOSEPH R. FORAND	ARTHUR F. FRAZIER	CLYDE W. FRAZIER
ESTY J. GALLANT	CARL V. GOSCINIAK	JAMES T. GUYETTE
CHARLES M. HAGER	TEODOR KOHUT	VALIER JANDREAU
RILEY M. JOHNSON	JOHN D. KANE	ANDREW KRATZ
RODNEY L'AMOUREUX	PAUL MASSIAN	CARL N. MEYERS
JOSEPH MOHAR	ALDACE B. NEWTON	ARTHUR J.C. NIELSON
JOSEPH OUELLETTE	JAMES E. PARKER	FRANKLIN H. PHILLIPS
WILMER D. RAMER	HORACE RAMSEY	HAROLD E. REED
LAURENTINO SANTANA	CHARLES H. SISSON	ARTHUR P. SMITH
JULIUS SOMBATI	MEYER SPIEGEL	CHARLES S. STEBBINS
ALADAR SZENTMILKLOSI	ROBERT E. TURNEY	JOHN F. BOOTH

PRIVATES

JACQUES BEAUCHESNE	PAUL BONGIORNO	UYLSSES J. BURCH
DELMAR CAIN	EUGENIO CASTIGLIONE	ANTHONY J. CHELKONIS
ALBERT H. CURRIER	CHARLES R. DAUGHERTY	CLYDE E. DeWITTE
GILBERT F. DUMAS	GEORGE A. HAHNE	JAMES T. HINES
NELSON J. HOPPER	BENJAMIN L. HOSTER	RAY T. HUMPHREY
ELWOOD S. HUNTLEY	DAVID W. KOEHL	LOUIS KOLOFOLOS
JOHN N. MIDDLEMAS	ELMER H. MILLER	LEONARD MILHAUSER
QUILLAN H. MOORE	GABRIEL MUCCI	MELVIN J. NEPTUNE
SAMUEL O. PARKER	ALVIN L. PIERCE	FREDERICK A. PRIMUS
VINCENT J. RADZAWIEZ	BYOD W. ROSE	HOWARD G. MEEKS
THOMAS F. MURPHY	ERNEST E. NIELSON	FREDERICK B. PASSINO
RAYMOND W. POLLOCK	DANIEL SARFATE	JAMES M. SICURANZA
THEODORE P. TREMBLAY	NICHOLAS SAPIEL	ARTHUR SOUZA
ARTHUR B. STOTT	THOMAS C. SPRINGFIELD	RAYMOND T. TREAT
DURWOOD WILKINSON	FRANK WOODCOCK	ELLERY C. CHRISTIE
*DAVID E. GOLDEN	RAYMOND L. COOPER	BEN F. KELLY
FORREST E. GOODE	GEORGE ASSAD	ADJUTOR BRETON
DONALD F. CHOATE	PAUL W. CRONIN	FRANKLIN CURTISS
KENNETH F. DAVIS	VINCENT J. DIEBALL	JOHN A. DOHERTY
LAWRANCE J. DOW	RALPH F. GOODENOUGH	ROBERT L. HARRIS

HOBART E. HARRISON   EARL R. HARVEY   LELAND F. HIGHMAN
FRANK C. HOOFFMAN   WILLIAM A. HOPKINS   EDWARD W. HIGGINS
BENJAMIN MISHLER   JOHN F. MURRAY   MICHAEL O'HARA
PASQUALE A. PESCE   GEORGE POTAMITIS   GEORGE SCIABARRA
GERALD J. SIROIS   AUGUSTINE ZONA   ROLAND E. JOSLYN
WALTER M. HOWSMAN   ROBERT E. HUTCHINS   FRANK A. INGENITO
RAYMOND L. JERDO   RICHARD L. JONES   BRUNO J. KANKOSKI
MORTIMER K. KARTEN   VICTOR KASHUBA   JOSEPH KASTELIC
LOUIS E. KECK   SAMUEL L. KESSLER   FLOYD E. KING
WILLIAM D. KELLY   HYMAN KRAVITZ   JOHN KRUSPER
PAUL E. LACOMBE   JOHN J. LALONE   SOL LEFKOWITZ
LOUIS L. LIPP   EARL F. LEGGUE   MORRIS LIFFMAN
BERNARD W. LUNDRIGAN JOSEPH J. LYONS   JOHN MAGGIROSARIO
    MANDIA
DONALD W. MAYO   MICHAEL P. McCARTHY   HAROLD J. McGRATH
JAMES P McNULTY   DANIEL J. MORAN   THOMAS B. NERO
JULIS OSTER   FRED C PLANTY   GEORGE F.
    RICHARDSON
FRANCIS E SHAW   ALLAN R. TORNBERG   MILTON BERMAN

COMPANY "E" ROSTER FEBRURY/MARCH 1945, ROER/RHINE VALLEYS, GERMANY. HEADQUARTERS, & FIELD TRAIN CAPTIAN PIERRE M. STEPANTIAN, COMMANDER

FIRST LIEUTENANTS
OWEN TEEVAN JR   G. BUCKWALTER

FIRST SERGEANT
VAUGHN E. MANNING

STAFF SERGEANTS
ELDRIDGE E. BENEFIELD   LAWRENCE L LEVITT   HILBERT

SERGEANTS
DeWITTE   EUGENE N VANN   DOBALD YERGAIN
CORPORAL BERLIN   T/5s HAROLD E. REED   ESTY E. GALANT
JOHN M. NORAK   ROBERT E. HUTCHINS   T/4s JOHN P BOOTH
FRANCIS J. LAUCHE   LEOPOLD FILA   JOHN F. MURRY
ERNEST E. ROACH

PRIVATES FIRST CLASS
WILLIAM SUN   EDGAR DRAPER   CHARLES BIGGS
EDWIN K. HANSSEN   ALFRED J. PISARSKI   CHARLES F. SNYDER
HARVEY L. WELLS   JOHN E. LAMDREAU   FRANK JONES
WAILBERT J. KROL   WALTER M. LACY   WILLIAM E.
    McCONATHY
CHARLES A. MURPHY   DEWEY E. WILLIAMS   CHERBA REED

FIRST PLATOON,

TECH SERGEANTS   FRANCISCO ANTOCICCO   EUGENE A. KEENAN

STAFF SERGEANTS,

EUGENE J. PFAFF	? EUGENE J. RAPP	CHARLES H SISSON
SERGEANT CECIL B. MARTIN	PRIVATES FIST CLASS, LARRY WOREB	OLE F. FISHER
JOE L. COTTEY	CHARLES L. WOOD	CLARENCE L. RINKA
NORMAN W. DAVIS	ROBERT J. GOODWIN	AAR0N L. ROMEL
LEE F. SANDEFUR	OTTAVIO POLITANO	SANDERS G HEBERT
EUGENE J. HATRIDGE	ROBERT H. NEEDHAM	HENRY R. PESCHEL
ELMER W. JONES	WILLIAM E. HOWER	WENZEL O STYGLES
ISAAC B. ALLEN	THOMAS P. McGUINNESS	WOODROW McMANUS
RAYMOND NEWTON	RAMER TERRES	WILLIE O'HAVER
VERNON R. KNIGHT	WILLIAM J. BOYD	WILLIAM M. RAMSEY
WILLIAM L. BEDNARE	LEE WILLIAMS	JACK A. SIMPSON
VERNON P. MULLER	ROBERT K. FELTER	WILLIAM T. JORDAN

SECOND PLATOON

TECH SERGEANT WILLIAM STELMA	STAFF SERGEANT ROBERT D. SERO	JAMES C. ROBERTS
SAMUEL H. SMITS	SERGEANT MANUEL	McLYNN SHARPE
CORPORAL EDWARD H. TIEKA	PRIVATE FIRST CLASS ERNEST MARX	HENRY SIKENMA
ANTHONY MIKIEWICZ	ARTHUR H. GLAZE	WILLIE J. RANKIN
EDWARD A. MACICEK	JAMES R. STUDDARDS	HENRY J. HUNT
WILLIAM J. KLIENE	WILLIAM D. KOSKOS	PARK L. BRADFORD
ROYAL A. ANDERSON	LEINARD F. UPSHAW	PRIVATS, JOHN T. KEENAN
JAMES L. MOORE	NOLAN L SANDERS	DONALD E. VAUTIER

THIRD PLATOON

SECOND LIEUTENANT EDWARD W. HIGGIN	TECH SERGEANT HENRY SMITH	STAFF SERGEANTS, JOHN L. McCORMICK
WENCESLAUS BERNACKI	SERGEANTS, ATLEE MESSCHER	KENNITH L. PADGETT
EDGER WELLS	HARRY P. HEHMEIETER	

PRIVATES FIRST CLASS

LONNIE B. MATTHEWS	WILLIAM J. NICHOLS	PAUL L. GARMAN
RAGNER O. LINDGREN	EMIL M. LINQUIST	NORMAN E. BENNETT
CECIL G. POWERS	THOMAS J. BLANKENBAKER	E. M. LOWE
LEE WILLIAMS	FLOYD S PHILLIPS	DONALD G. HOLMES
MAURICE L. SCALES	LESLIE L. BEERS	ROLAND L. REVIER
ODELL W. JONES	MATTHEW J. MULLIGAN	ROYAL ANDERSON
MAJCHROWSKI	CORPORAL CARTER PALMER	LENES C. JONES
ROBERT KIEWATT	WAY SUTTEN	CARL A. RAVIN
CHARLES W. ARMES	CHARLES W. KRAUTER	JAMES L. McAFEE

FRANK R. KRIEBEL
CHRLES W. PARKER
DONALD S. HELMES
LONES C. JONES
T/5 JAMES B. MYRICK
T/4 LEROY M. SEYMOUR

PHILLIP D. DAREST
JOHN L. WICHARD
HOSA L. AVERS
RODNEY B. HUNT
FRED O. JENKINS

JAMES D. OSBORNE
THOMAS J. CASTRO
GEORGE J. LENSKY
THOMAS J. JOYCE
CHARLES E ARMES

FOURTH PLATOON

FIRST LIEUTENANT
JOHN K. SNODEN

TECH SERGEANT
SAMUEL D. SPIVEY

STAFF SERGEANTS

FRED PREVOST
SERGEANTS, JIMMIE E.
  LITCHFIELD
JAMES E. HASS
CORPORAL AUBREY
  McGARRAHAM

DONALD H. VOSS
WALTER E. LINDSTROM

HARRY H. REMBRENT

JOSEPH T. HERBERT
DELMAR P. RICHARDS

CHESTER MOORE

PRIVATES FIRST CLASS

WALTER D. KEELER
ABERNATHY C.
  CARPENTER
JAMES B. MASON

DAVID R. GREGORY
JAMES R. VALONE
CLETUS H. FAUBER
DOMININO J. POLZELLA
PRIVATES, JASON JOY

MORRIS G. CRUM
HENRY V. HIDER

JOHN POLOVITCH

JOSEPH STROUB
IRVIN L. HICKMAN
LOUIS R. JULIAN
GEORGE S. HICKS
HENERY A. HESSE

ARTHUR E. LaBOUFF
ISOM M. BOWLING

GARDNER O.
  HARRISON
FRANK C. CONNER
ROBERT L. FERBES
EMERICK
HAROLD J. McGRATH
BENKO

The Fighting First,
Brief History in WWII *
(Written October 1944)

The units of the Division have a long and distinguished history from 1776, and served in peace and war. (The last wartime service was in Saudi Arabia and Kuwait. Only WWII will be discussed in this Narrative).

Although the First Division comprises some of the oldest units in the American Army, the Division itself was not formed until nineteen seventeen in France. Historically, the oldest organization is Battery D, of the 5th FA Battalion. Battery D was the entire army shortly after the Revolution; the rest of the Continental Army had been disbanded by a previous Congress because of the expenses of maintenance. Battery D was organized by Alexander Hamilton in 1776 and fought in the Battle of Long Island.

During the first World War, the Division was the first U.S. Army division to land in France, the first to suffer casualties, and the first to take prisoners. It participated in the battle of Cantigny, the first full-scale American offensive, and later in the campaigns of Picardy Montdidier-Noyons, Aisne-Marne, St. Michiel, MueseArgonne, Lorraine, Soissons and the Argonne. The 26th Infantry was the first American Infantry Regiment to enter Germany (on 1 December 1918) as part of the army of occupation. In WWII, advance elements sailed for England on 1 July nineteen forty-two and the entire Division was overseas and garrisoned in England by 9 August 1942.

The Division had been picked as one of the assaulting forces for the invasion of North Africa and the capture of Oran. Amphibious training for the invasion was conducted in Scotland during September and October. On 8 November 1942 the Division landed two forces on either side of Oran; the 16th and 18th Infantry went ashore at

Arzew, and the 26th Infantry in the vicinity of Les Andalouses. After the fall of Oran, the Division was committed piecemeal in the long and confused advance across Algeria and Tunisia. Units of the Division operating under various commands participated in the battles of Tebourba, Medjez-el-Rab and Longstop Hill. During the operation in the Qusseltia Valley, which began twenty January 1943, there, the Division made its only withdrawal of the war. A move which was dictated by a German breakthrough in another part of the line rather than any enemy pressure. This breakthrough was the opening stage of the battles for the Kasserine Pass. Late in February 1943, the First Division launched a crushing counterattack to hold the Pass and was successful in driving the Germans back and inflicting heavy losses.

After relief by the 9th U.S. Infantry Division on 27 February, the Division reorganized, attacked, and took Gafsa after a spectacular 40-mile motor march. During subsequent operations in the vicinity of now famous El Guettar, the Division withstood and drove back four full-scale tank and infantry attack by the German 10th Panzer Division. Later, the Division moved North in the vicinity of Reja and engaged in the bitter operations which finally resulted in the fall of Mateur. During these battles, the Division was opposed by the famous German "Barenthin" Regiment. On 7 May, the day Tunis fell, the Division was relieved. Preparations for the invasion of Sicily were made in the vicinity of Oran, and on 10 July the Division attacked the beaches of Gela. Gela was quickly taken, but the enemy made a strong, coordinated counterattack during which their tanks approached to within 1,000 yards of the beach. The Division stood its ground, and on the following day the advance continued. On 1 August, Troina was captured after savage fighting. During the battle the 16th Infantry repulsed seven counterattacks, the 18th Infantry one, and 26th Infantry, thirteen. The Division was relieved about the middle of August and reorganized at Palme Di Montecharo. On 23 October, the First Division sailed for England, arriving 5 November.

Soon after the Division's arrival in England, Division Headquarters began blocking out plans for the invasion of France. Preparations included intensive training in assault tactics, street fighting, river crossings, reduction of pillboxes and strong points and amphibious landings. On six June nineteen forty-four, the Division struck at the beaches near Colleville-Sur-Mer in the face of intensive small-arms fire and mortar and artillery concentrations laid down by a full strength German division which had moved into the area two days before for anti-invasion maneuvers. After a temporary stalemate on the beach itself, the Division broke through the crust of the enemy defenses. During the ensuing three days, the 352nd German Infantry Division was overrun and destroyed as the Division drove South, halting its advance at Caumont, the farthest Southern penetration of the Normandy beachhead. The advance was stopped at Caumont until friendly units on either side of the Division could come up and cover the Division's dangerously exposed flanks. The friendly units never did pull abreast, but in spite of an enemy counterattack to retake Caumont on 15 and 16 June, the First Division held firm until relieved by the 5th Infantry Division in the middle of July.

On 13 July, the Division moved to Colombieres to refit and reequip for the assault which was to break the containing forces holding the Allies in the beachhead area. The plan called for the Division to pass through the 9th Division in the center of the Cotentin Peninsula base, capture Marigny and continue the advance to Coutances on the West. On 27 July, Marigny fell and the Division continued its offensive South and West.

South of Coutances, the Division cut Eastward again and took the high ground East of Mortain. The purpose of this operation was to hold open the supply corridor down the Western side of the Cotentin Peninsula through Coutances and Avranches, and its result was the now famous "Falaise pocket." Although the first Division did not receive most all the force of the German counterattack to close the supply route, the situation East of Mortrain produced a curious tactical situation. As the First Division expanded its position with the aid of an attached CT from the 9th Infantry Division, it was engaged on three sides. The CT from the 9th Division was attacking North, the main body of the Division was moving South toward Mayenne, and the left flank off the Division was under steady pressure from the East. Mayaenne fell on 6 August.

The Division then turned Northeast and drove to LaFerte Mace. From there, the First Division moved Eastward. Three days after the First Division reconnaissance had felt out the situation on the Seine, the First Division itself had crossed the river and taken Meaux on the Marne. Two days later Soissons fell — Soissons, where the Division had lost nine thousand men in four days, a quarter of a century before. For Major General Clarence Huebner, it was the second campaign through the area. In the last war, he commanded a battalion in the First Division; this time he commanded the First Division itself. On 14 August, Division engineers were blowing up pillboxes on the Chemin-dess-Dames between Soissons and Laon; the Germans were pulling out too fast to attempt to defend them with any tenacity. As the First Division attacked Northwards toward Mons in the first days of September, it ran directly into the flank of a German corps trying desperately to extricate itself Eastward to the Siegfried Line on the Mons-Liege Road.

The ensuing battles resulted in one of the most catastrophic defeats the German Army suffered in France. All elements of the First Division including Division Headquarters, the First Division Artillery and the Engineers were engaged in close combat. More than seventeen thousand prisoners were taken in four days by the First Division alone, and the Third Armored Division, operating on the First Division's right, took additional thousands. German dead and wounded ran into the thousands, and with this defeat, German hopes of holding the Siegfried Line in strength in the Aachen area collapsed; it was apparent that the forces caught at Mons had been racing to the West Wall to man it before the Allies got there.

Four divisions were largely destroyed by the First Division at Mons and two others ground down to skeletons. After the Mons Battles, the Division encountered only moderate opposition in its rapid advance through Belgium, Charleroi, Namur and Liege fell in quick succession. Finally, on 12 September, advance patrols of the Division crossed the last frontier of the European war, passing into Germany proper some six kilometers East of Aachen. The deployment of First Division forces that day was international; there was a reinforced battalion in Germany, an outpost in Holland, the main body of the First Division in Belgium and rear echelon in France. After two hours of hard fighting, the first belt of the Siegfried Line West of Aachen had been forced; on 15 September, three days later, East of Aachen, the second and last closely-knit line of fortifications and pillboxes were breached.

In this war, as in the last, the First Division has maintained its tradition of being the first in every operation. It was the first infantry division to land in Africa, Sicily, the first to land in France, the first to break out of the Normandy beachhead, the first to force the Siegfried Line. Since the original landing in Africa, the First Division has captured more than 47,500 prisoners, most of them in France and Belgium. This does not include the tens of thousands who surrendered at the end of the Tunisian Campaign.

DOUGHBOY
Origin and Intriguing Mystery *

The first theory says the earliest written reference to "doughboy" is in a book published in 1816. The tale is of some three hundred buccaneers who landed on the Atlantic Coast of Panama in 1660. They were each issued four doughboy cakes before their march across the Isthmus of Panama to the Pacific Coast.

The second says that white was the Infantry color before blue. Infantry officers in the 1860s wore white horse hair plumes flying from their spiked parade helmets. White wool insets or shoulder boards identified the wearer as an Infantryman. Enlisted men had white cord on the facing of their uniforms. In an effort to keep the uniforms looking sharp, the Infantrymen would dampen their white clay smoking pipes and rub the white clay paste on their uniforms to cover up a dirty spot on the white uniform facing. The clay pipes looked like dough.

The third theory says the name came from the large, round jacket buttons that Infantrymen wore following the Civil War. The buttons looked like dough.

Fourth explanation is that the word came from the mud the Infantryman marched through. The mud took on the consistency of bread dough.

Dr. Noah Webster says, DOUGHBOY is a nickname of the United States Infantry Soldier.

It means, an infantryman that gives honorable service, noble traditions, the will to do, and the ability to win.

Regardless of the origin of the word DOUGHBOY," it has always been associated with the Infantryman, dependable, with the cunning knowledge to survive, that's the "DOUGHBOY."

* The Staff of The National Infantry Museum and Webster's Dictionary.

French and Belguim Fourrageres *
Theories of Origin

There are some logical and factual theories of the origin of fourrageres. First, as a forage rope, a long cord was fastened around the neck then wrapped twice around the body. Then from the right shoulder to the left hip and finally on the chest where it ended with two large plaits and tassels. Later the cord became a simple ornament of the uniform in fashion of a braided cord fastened to the left shoulder by a double tassel on the chest at the second vest button.

Another version is that a Flemish regiment retreated and the Duke of Albe to show his dissatisfaction decided that in the future the punishment for men of that regiment would consist of torture on the gallows. The Flemish stung to the quick, replied proudly they would from then on wear on their shoulder a rope and nail so they would always be ready to be hung. Since that time they distinguished themselves on the battle field, thus the rope and nail of disgrace became a glorious insignia in which other regiments envied.

Still another version is during the reign of Napoleon a regiment was ordered to defend at all costs a key position. The commanding officer ordered his men to hang themselves before surrender, they distinguished themselves, thus, they requested that they be permitted to wear a rope and nail on their uniforms as a symbol of distinction.

STORY TIME,
March/April 1945

Quick Fix: *

The story of today is about the two Nazi soldiers talking. One of them said he had a secret weapon that would bring the war to a quick finish. "Vot iss it, Fritz?" asked his pal excitedly. "A white flag on a long pole," was the reply.

GI Rodeo *

A really wild "western front" rodeo was staged by the men of Company E. Headquarters. It all happened during one of these unaccountable lulls when Jerry seems to have used his ration of mortar shells for the day. First Sergeant Manning, of Paris, Texas, who has ridden in many rodeos emerged from his dugout and overheard a group of drugstore cowboys discussing the pros and cons of roping steers and riding broncos. Manning interjected the comment that probably none of them could even ride the sheep that were grazing near by. This raised the curtain on the show and Private. Sun and Private Hickman mounted two of the noble animals and put on a magnificent exhibition, lunging, leaping and plunging across the pasture like full-fledged range riders. Manning conceded that the riding was well done and thought the incident closed. But the sheep had different ideas. One of the sheep kept his eye on the Sergeant, and when that worthy stooped over, the fuzzy wuzzy took a running start and rammed the Sergeant in the seat. It was just plain justice we call it. It may be of interest to note that Pvt. Sun from Springfield, Ohio and Pvt. Hickman from West Plains, Missouri, were still limping.

FAIR ENOUGH *

Most of the men of E Company slept in straw while at Eudenbach. Noticed quite a few of them scratching today. Sgt. Jimmy Litchfield was examining himself through a magnifying glass, "Let's take a look," someone asked. Litchfield turned to him in disgust and said, "Gwan, it's my louse, if you want to see, get your own louse."

Erft Canal is Jumped *

The First Battalion came into action again to overrun Rleisheim at the Erft Canal. The Second Bn. at the same time was employed in taking Rlessham and Liblar. Liblar was secured after the destruction of several pillboxes and antitank guns, but a vicious counterattack was immediately launched with SPs and tanks spearheading the German Infantry. However, the American TDs took care of all the enemy tanks and SPs and the attack was beaten off. During the battle one tank had approached to within twenty yards of Col. Daniel's CP, who had a similar experience once before at Butgenbach. Next day the men of the Second Bn. left their billets at Schloss Gracht for Bruhl, which fell without opposition. While the First Bn. occupied Pingsdorf and Rlue took Schwandorf and Watchburg, E. Co. went on to clear Rerzdorf, setting up outposts on the Rhine. For the second time in a generation, the First Division had established its Watch on the Rhine.

*The SPADE and, The American Traveler, and unknown sources.

A DOUGHBOY'S NARRATIVE

An ideal gift for the enthusiast of History and the depression of the thirties, the war years and the fifties.

A book of non-fiction wartime experiences, of good taste, and very interesting to all.

To order more copies of

A Doughboy's Narrative

Call: 1-912-432-8810

Or write to:

SAMUEL D. SPIVEY
3621 COUNCIL ROAD
ALBANY, GEORGIA 31705-9006

Everyone has a difference in evaluations and opinions, I would appreciate yours. Would you please share with us your comments on this book, "A Doughboy's Narrative." Send comments to.

SAMUEL D. SPIVEY
3621 Council Road
Albany, Georgia 31705-9006

Spring 1941, myself with some of the fearless 4th Platoon teammates. Front center, me, front standing, center three are Phillips, Peschel, Cunliffe, I don't remember the names of the rest; or rather, in these group pictures I become confused, and I am not sure that I can match names and faces correctly, so I won't try.

Tipton and I young soldiers, good friends and happy, summer 1940. Near the main gate of Fort Devens. As I reminisce of back then I remember the tranquillity, the beauty, joy, and happy feelings that is hard to explain. Then in 1942 began the horrible, dreadful miserable times in Africa, Sicily, France, Belgium, and Germany. (and so was Korea).

Fort Devens, Spring 1941, Frazier and I playing soldier while on local maneuvers. Men that one has served in combat with is a special person, one that you will never ever forget. Frazier, Miller, Kessler, Mock, and a few others is very, very special in my heart. When I think of them that gave all, I choke, and have tears.

Early spring 1941, rough, tough, heros, Mock, Frazier, Cunliffe, my best friends, and my best buddies, and the best doughboys ever.

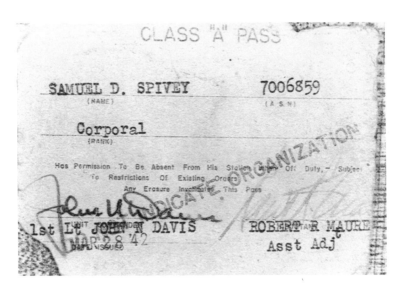

A class "A" pass meant many privileges and was highly treasured.

Fort Devens 1941, Company E 26th Infantry

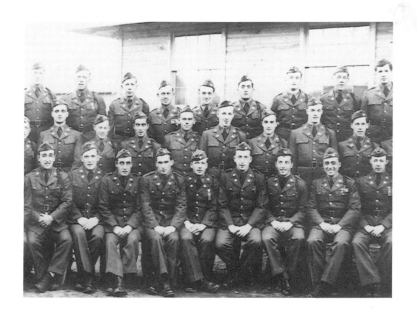

Fort Devens 1941, Company E 26th Infantry

Fort Devens 1941, Company E 26th Infantry

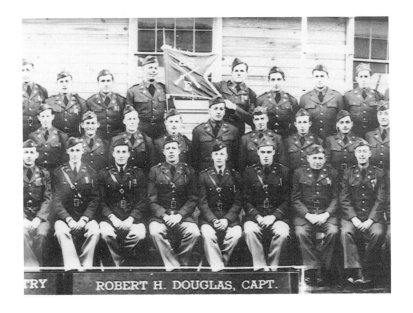

Fort Devens 1941, Company E 26th Infantry

Fort Devens 1941, Company E 26th Infantry

Fort Devens 1941, Company E 26th Infantry

Fort Devens 1941, Company E 26th Infantry. Some members were
on leave, or on duty and not in the picture. At our reunions we try to
name these comrades and I admit that we name for certain only a
few. August of 44 when I was knocked out of action there was only
a few still in the Company. Last of March 45 there were maybe three
or so.

North Africa 43, DeWitte and Reed two more of the tough, fearless teammates and friends.

North Africa 43, I don't remember if I had been a bad boy or not, Reed using a sword as a pointer playing professor.

Taken in Brounemouth, England, February, 1944. On pass and having a marvelous time, Miller, one the best buddies I ever had, we tried not to worry about our future.

Still trying to live life at it's fullest and with no remorse, loose as a goose, brainless, and happy.

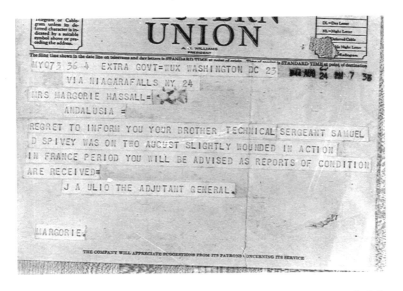

Telegram to my sister, Margie Spivey Hassell saying, "just slightly wounded", maybe they were right, yet I was in the hospital almost five months.

Me and another one of the fearless Doughboys, Antocicco, wounded three times. He and I returned to States at the same time, we left Germany the last of March 1945. A dedicated friend that could always be counted on to do his best.

February 1944. Fifty years ago I knew the names of these men as well as my own, and I apologize for not remembering all of their names; they, Doughboy combat veterans and heros, my friends, my buddies, my teammates, and my men, the 4th Platoon. Sitting, Keeler, Polovich, Crum, Lindstrom, Berlin, standing, Valone, Spivey, Hieder or Mason, Voss. Near the Roer River and we were waiting for the water to recede so that we could cross the Roer.

Fort Benning 1952. Just returned home after a Saturday morning Inspection.

Retirement Ceremony, Fort McPherson, Ga. May 1965. Going into civilian life was sorta a shock.

May, Beta, and I, Pittsburg. We really enjoy getting re-acquainted with our friends.

L'Amoureux, Richardson, Diem, Spiegel, and Neumann, Pittsburg.

L'Amoureux, Manning, DeWitte, Neumann, Spiegel. sitting; standing, Diem, Spivey, Mortimer, Richardson, Oster.

Sitting, Florence Spiegel, Florence Oster, L'Amoureux, Spivey, Euvida(Beta) Spivey, Neumann, Dorothy Neumann; standing, Richardson, Cartier, Oster, Spiegel.

Cartier, Belisle, Spivey, Neumann. standing, Oster, Dieball.

Dorothy Neumann, Mary Spivey, my sister-in-law and I, Pittsburg.

Fort McPherson, Ga. August 64, Receiving the Army Commendation Medal, August 1964.

All dressed for a WWII Commemorative Program, Albany, 1993.

Tegucigalpa, Honduras 56. Some of the good life, Euvida and me off to a fling at the US Embassy. Times like these we appreciated.

Son James David Spivey, a hero, a living legend in his time. Served his Country above and beyond of what is required. He served in the Navy as Submariner, in the Army as a Paratrooper, and had a distinguished career in the U.S. Army Special Forces.

Number One daughter Cathy, husband Jeff Barrett, their son Ben, and daughter Meredith.

Number Two daughter Debbie, husband Steve Lunsford, their son Andrew, and daughter Erin. Beta and I are very proud of our Son, daughters, son-in-laws, and grand children. They are the joy, that makes life worth living.